Raster Reclamation based Inferometric Analectic of Visograph

Melech Osher

Raster Reclamation based Inferometric Analectic of Visograph

First Edition October 2025

Written by Melech Osher

Contents

CHAPTER-1

INTRODUCTION

Today, vast collections of digital images are available across the world. To make effective use of these databases, efficient and reliable image retrieval techniques are essential. Traditionally, images were retrieved using text-based annotations, where each image was manually labeled and later searched through keywords. However, with the rapid growth in both the number and variety of images, this approach has become inefficient and often ambiguous.

As a result, Content-Based Image Retrieval (CBIR) has gained significant attention. Since the early 1990s, CBIR has emerged as a vital area of research within the multimedia community, focusing on retrieving images directly based on their visual features rather than text descriptions. The rise of digital storage has led to massive repositories of unlabeled image data—stored both on the web and within networked systems—making automated image retrieval an increasingly important challenge.

The widespread availability of smartphones and digital cameras has further accelerated the production of images, increasing the need for intelligent retrieval methods. Search engines such as Google, Bing, and Flickr now invest heavily in improving image search capabilities. Yet, one of the main obstacles remains the lack of consistent or accurate textual information for these images. Human labeling is often subjective, and different annotators may describe or interpret the same image in varying ways. This inconsistency highlights the necessity for robust, content-based approaches that rely on visual analysis rather than manual description.

To overcome these limitations, Content Based Image Retrieval (CBIR) was proposed in the early 1990*s*. *In the recent past, Google has launched a new application, called "Google Goggles" for Google Android mobile phones*[1]*, which is a content-based search application and allows people to search for more information about a famous landmark or work of art simply by taking a photo of that object.*

CBIR systems create machine-interpretable descriptions of an image's physical characteristics such as color, texture, shape etc. These descriptions, known as extracted features, can then be compared by a measure of similiarity. The similarity between a given query image and every image in the image archive is then computed by CBIR system, and finally ranks the images in the collection according to their degree of relevance to the user's query.

Even after designing several compact and efficient features vector for indexing each image, still there remains a wide gap between actual human perceptions model with that of feature based model used for CBIR. This is mainly due to the fact that the design of feature vector is solely based on low level visual information (like color, texture, shape etc.) without taking into account the semantic information like spatial organization, context, events etc. To overcome this shortcoming and in trying to incorporate certain amount of visual perception characteristic in the feature vector design, people have proposed the relevance feedback mechanism in CBIR design with active participation of human observers.

Images are being generated at an ever increasing rate, by sources such as defence and civilian satellites, military reconnaissance and surveillance flights, fingerprinting and mug-shot-capturing devices, scientific experiments, biomedical imaging, and home entertainment systems. Application areas in which CBIR has a principal activity are numerous and diverse: art galleries, law enforcements and criminal investigation, interior design, trademark and copyright database management, remote sensing and management of earth resources, scientific database management, weather forecasting, retailing, fabric and fashion design, Medical Imaging and picture archiving and communication systems. With the recent interest in multimedia systems, CBIR has attracted the attention of researchers across several disciplines.

1.1 A BRIEF REVIEW OF CBIR SYSTEMS

One of the major building blocks of a CBIR system is the feature extraction block. In the feature extraction block, an image is represented by features which allow searching for images similar to a given image. A feature is defined to capture a certain visual property of an image. Color, texture, shape, etc. are the most widely used features in CBIR applications. Several CBIR algorithms have been developed using only single features. A single feature normally describes a specific aspect of the image content. Therefore multiple visual features are necessary for the general purpose CBIR. Recent research work uses multiple visual features, which can improve the retrieval performance effectively. Various multiple visual feature extraction schemes have been used in the literature to find the low-dimensional salient and significant features, which can effectively be used to represent the underlying image's visual characteristics. The most commonly used features in designing CBIR system are color, texture, shape, and keypoint descriptor. Brief discussion about each of which will be presented in the following paragraph. Besides that, descriptions about some commercially available CBIR system will also be presented.

Different color features in CBIR systems: The color signature of object in the foreground and also that of background makes it as one of the important vision ques. Color is considered to be a robust visual feature because it is invariant to direction, size, rotation and shift. Point/pixel and block/group based are the two different color representation schemes. Pixel based color representation includes color moments and Color Co-occurrence Matrix (CCM), where color histogram and color correlogram comes under block/group based representation schemes.

In general, color spaces are classified into linear color spaces and non-linear color spaces. The RGB color space is an additive color space based on three primary colors: red, green and blue. Secondary colors can be generated by using the primary colors. However, the RGB space is not very efficient in dealing with real-world images, thus it is avoided in most of the image retrieval algorithms because it lacks the ability of measuring the perceptual similarity. Accordingly, the HSV color space is used instead of the RGB color space because the components of hue and saturation are very close to human visual perception. The HSV model has three constituent components *i.e.*, the "hue" which refers the color, the "saturation" which refers the "vibrancy" of the color, and the "value" which refers the brightness of the color. As another color space, the YCbCr color space is divided into luminance (Y) and chrominance (Cb, Cr), while Cb and Cr denote the blue yellow and red-green color difference, respectively. The *L* a* b* color space is also derived from the XYZ color space to achieve perceptual uniformity. As in YCbCr, *L* a* b* consists of one lightness dimension (L) and two chrominance dimensions (*a*, b**) based on the color opponent process.

Color histogram is a popular color representation that has been used in many image retrieval systems. Its performance in characterizing global color content has been widely recognized. However, color histograms lacks the information about the spatial distribution of color; thus, other representations such as color correlogram and auto-correlogram have been proposed. These methods provide information about the changes of the spatial correlation of color pairs with the distance in an image, and they have shown better retrieval performance than color histograms. In addition, many algorithms have been proposed in the CBIR domain based on color moments. The key idea of color moments is the use of standard deviation and mean of distributions in each color band as a color feature. This is considered as a compact characteristic and therefore it is usually used as an optimization process along with other color features. Xiaoyin *et al.* have proposed a new color image retrieval method using the color moment invariant. Representative colors are computed for each image instead of being fixed in a given color space, thus this allows feature representation to be more accurate and compact. The proposed method is based on small image descriptors and adaptive to the context of the image itself by two-stage clustering approach.

CCM and Motif Co-occurrence Matrix (MCM) were developed by employing the spatial relation between color channels. An image can be considered as a composition of suitable "elementary structures". The elements of those pixels carry visual attributes, i.e. colors, and possess relations, i.e. distances between them. Accordingly, image contents can be characterized by an appropriate M-dimensional CCM where the attributes and relation-ships are represented by different matrix axes. Guoping has proposed the Block Truncation Coding (BTC) as a different image coding technique which was employed in the CBIR for compressing color images. From the BTC compressed stream without decoding, two description features of image content was derived: Block Color Co-occurrence Matrix (BCCM) and Block Pattern Histogram (BPH). Both BCCM and BPH were used to compute the similarity measures of images for CBIR applications. Nowadays, some BCT variants have been proposed for CBIR tasks. The Scalable Color Descriptor (SCD), Color Layout Descriptor (CLD), Color Structure Descriptor (CSD) and Dominant Color Descriptor (DCD) have widely been applied in image retrieval applications of Moving Picture Expert Group (MPEG)-7 color descriptors. Recently, Zeng *et al.* employed the Color Coherence Vector (CCV) based on the distance histogram. They also proposed a multiscale Distance Coherence Vector (DCV) algorithm in accordance with problems where different shapes have the same descriptor and the poor performance of anti-noise of image retrieval algorithm based on the DCV. This algorithm obtains relatively smoother contour curves by Gaussian function evolving contour curve, and then calculates the DCV of the original contour curve and evolved contour curves. This algorithm is invariant to the translation, rotation, and scaling transformations.

Different texture features in CBIR systems: Although texture plays an important role in image processing and computer vision task, but unfortunately, there is no precise definition of the notion texture. Petrou *et al.* define texture has the variation of data at scales smaller than the scales of interest. Generally speaking, textures are complex visual patterns composed of entities, or sub-patterns that have characteristic brightness, directionality, coarseness, randomness, fineness, smoothness, granulation, slope, size, etc. Thus texture can be regarded as a similarity grouping in an image. Hence, texture is an important feature for describing innate surface properties of a particular object and its relationship with the surrounding regions in an image. However, the computation complexity and retrieval accuracy are the main challenging drawbacks of texture-based CBIR systems.

Many texture-based image retrieval methods were proposed in CBIR. Some commonly used texture queues are texture descriptor based on Gabor filters, Wavelet transforms, Gray-Level Co-occurrence Matrix (GLCM), Markov Random Field (MRF), Edge Histogram Descriptor (EHD), Steerable Pyramid Decomposition (SPD), and Tamura features. Gabor filters are set of wavelets and each wavelet captures energy at a specific frequency and orientation. Gabor wavelet transforms have multi-resolution and multi-orientation properties and this is optimal for measuring local spatial frequencies. Many transform-based feature extraction techniques are used including Discrete Wavelet Transform (DWT), Curvelet Transform (CVT), Contourlet Transform (CNT), Non-sub sampled Contourlet Transform (NSCT), Ripplet Transform (RT) etc. These transform are used to extract low-level features due to its superiority in multi-resolution/geo-metric analysis and spatial frequency.

Recently, some works in CBIR paradigm have been carried out either by using a single descriptor or by combining many algorithms to form a robust descriptor for image texture. Liu *et al.* have developed a new image retrieval approach, namely Micro-Structure Descriptor (MSD). However, MSD model has not simulated visual attention mechanisms well. Therefore, to address this problem, recently a novel computational visual-attention model, namely salient structure model, for CBIR has been proposed in Kwitt *et al.* introduced a probabilistic based texture model image retrieval. It is based on some statistical measurement done on image representation in complex wavelet domain. There are several other statistical based texture modeling is developed in.

Different shape features in CBIR systems: Like color and textures, the shape is another fundamental unit of perception which carries semantic information of an image. Shape feature can be categorized into two groups namely contour-based and region based approach. In contour-based approach, features are computed from outer boundary while region based approach features are extracted from the entire region.

Shape analysis is a well-explored research area with many shape representation and similarity measurement techniques found in the literature. Generally, shape descriptors are used with other features such as color and texture and tend to be efficient in specific applications such as for retrieval of man-made objects. Shape features can be extracted using various methods such as Fourier descriptors, B-splines, Curvature Scale Space (CSS), etc.

Generally, contour-based shape methods require a high computation time in obtaining the correspondence between contour points from two shapes using local contour in-formation respectively. In order to solve this problem, Shu *et al.* proposed a new contour-based descriptor for closed curves, namely the Contour Points Distribution Histogram (CPDH), which depicts the deformable potential at each point along a curve. In addition, developed a ground distance calculation technique, which is based on the Earth Mover's Distance (EMD) under polar coordinates, for shape matching in order to be in-variant to scale and translation. Another approach, that combines the contour-based and region-based shape methods, is proposed by Chen and Xu, namely the rolling penetrate descriptor. This method improves the conventional methods by obtaining any desired in-formation in a unified way rather than in a specific aspect of shape features.

In region based techniques, all the pixels within a shape region are taken into account to obtain the shape representation. Common region based methods use moment descriptors to describe shape. These include geometric moments, Legendre moments, Zernike moments and pseudo Zernike moments. Several researchers also use the grid method to describe shape. Since region-based shape representations combine information across an entire object rather than exploiting information just at boundary points, they can capture interior information in a shape. Other advantages of region-based methods are, it can be employed to describe disjoint shape and robust to shape distortions. Bronstein *et al.* developed an interesting approach for extracting the shape feature, namely the Shape Google. This approach was proposed in the context of non-rigid shape retrieval, and inspired by the work of Ovsjanikov *et al.* who first introduced this approach.

Different key points descriptors in CBIR systems: It describes local information using key points of some image parts such as region, object of interest, edges, or corners. Recently, key point descriptors have shown their superiority for various types of applications in computer vision, as well as in CBIR paradigm. Key point descriptors have many advantages over traditional global features since they are invariant to image scale and rotation, and provide robust matching across a wide range of different situations. As the research attention in CBIR context has shifted to use these key points features, a comprehensive review of different key point descriptors are presented.

Scale-Invariant Feature Transform (SIFT) is one of the most successful and widely applied key points descriptors in the last decade. The SIFT is very robust for extracting distinct invariant features from images in order to carry out reliable matching between different views of objects or scenes. Many CBIR system using SIFT and its variants have been reported in the literature.

In 2008, a new robust key point feature detector was introduced by Bay *et al.*, namely Speeded Up Robust Features (SURF). One major drawback of SIFT descriptor is it high dimensionality, and applying Principal Component Analysis (PCA) in PCA-SIFT and Gradient Location and Orientation Histogram (GLOH) slows down the feature computation. This descriptor is partly inspired by the SIFT descriptor so the authors have claimed that the standard SURF is faster than SIFT and more robust against different image transformations.

The bag-of-words (BoW) feature is generally based on tokenizing keypoint-based descriptor, like, SIFT; to generate a visual-word vocabulary / codebook. Then, the visual-word vector of an image contains the presence or absence information of each visual word in the image.For example, the number of keypoints in the corresponding cluster is a visual word. Since last decade, BoW has been used extensively in an image an-notation [94]. However, computing the BoW representation for an image is tedious and the computation time grows linearly with the size of the codebook. Although BoW model provides good accuracy for image search, it is not scalable for large image databases, as it is intensive both in memory and computations. In order to have a more informative image representation, Peronnin *et al.* proposed a generative model based approach called Fisher Vector (FV). They estimate a parametric probability distribution over the feature space from a huge representative set of features, generally a Gaussian Mixture Model (GMM). The GMM can be interpreted as a probabilistic visual vocabulary, where each Gaussian forms a visual word or cluster. Compared to the BoW, which only records the count of local descriptors in each visual word, the FV encodes the higher order statistics, resulting in a more discriminative representation and hence better performance.

Jegou *et al.*, proposed Vector of Locally Aggregated Descriptors (VLAD) as a non-probabilistic equivalent to FV. VLAD is a simplified and special case of Fisher vector, in which the residuals belonging to each of the code words are accumulated. The concatenated residuals represent the image, using which the search is carried out via simple distance measures. A number of improvements have been proposed to make VLAD a better representation by considering vocabulary adaptation and intra-normalization, residual normalization and local coordinate system, geometry information and multiple vocabularies. In, the VLAD vectors are L2 normalized. Subsequently, a signed square rooting (SSR) normalization was introduced following its use for Fisher vectors. To obtain the SSR normalized VLAD, each element of an un-normalized VLAD is sign square rooted and the transformed vector is L2 normalized. The main weakness of VLAD is its partial robustness to outliers. A single outlier descriptor located far from the cluster center can outweigh the combined contribution from many inlier descriptors located close to that center.

Local Binary Pattern (LBP) is widely used feature description method. It was introduced for the texture classification by Ojala *et al.* and shown its utility in area of image retrieval. Various variants of the LBP also exist in the literature such as a Local Derivative Patterns (LDPs), Local Ternary Pattern (LTP), Center Symmetric Local Binary Pattern (CSLBP), Center Symmetric Local Ternary Pattern (CSLTP), etc. However, LBP, LDP, and LTP extract the information based upon the distribution of edges which are coded by only two directions (*e.g.*, positive or negative). To improve the performance of these methods, Local Tetra Patterns (LTrPs) was introduced in the CBIR domain. Local Mesh Pattern (LMeP) and Local Ternary Co-occurrence Pattern (LTCoP) are the recent feature description methods for de-signing CBIR system. Recently, LDEP is introduced in order to overcome the few short coming of LBP and different modified LBP methods.

In general, some of above mentioned key points descriptors are computed on the dense grid of uniformly spaced cells and their performance is improved using overlapping local contrast normalization. Dalal and Friggs proposed locally normalized Histograms of Oriented Gradients (HOG) descriptors to provide better performance compared to other existing features including wavelets. Chandrasekhar *et al.* proposed another alternative descriptor, namely the Compressed Histogram of Gradients (CHoG), as a low bit-rate descriptor with a 20 times reduction in the bit rate.

Another key point descriptor employed in the CBIR domain is Difference Between Pixels of Scan Pattern (DBPSP), which mainly calculates the differences among all pixels within motifs of a scan pattern. Usually it is combined with other image features and used as texture feature as described. As an alternative to SIFT and SURF, Rublee *et al.* had introduced a binary descriptor called the Oriented fast and Rotated Brief (ORB), which is based on FAST detector and BRIEF descriptor. In 2011, a new key point descriptor called Binary Robust Invariant Scalable Key-points (BRISK) is introduced by Leutenegger *et al.* Fast Retina Key-point (FREAK) descriptor is a very recent developed by Alahi *et al.* It is inspired by the Human Visual System (HVS), or more precisely, by the retina. Recently, a new descriptor called Nested Shape Descriptor (NSD) has been proposed. This is the first binary descriptor to outperform SIFT on the standard VGG-Affine benchmark. Furthermore, the NSD binary descriptor significantly outperforms BRISK, a state-of-the-art binary descriptor.

Different distance measure used in CBIR systems: The similarity/dissimilarity measure between images is second major important blocks in the CBIR system after the feature extraction. To achieve more accurate retrieval and better performance, the CBIR system should employ an efficient similarity measure that can accurately model the similarity distance in perceptual space. Finding out a suitable distance measure which can capture more accurately human perception mechanism is a challenging research issue.

Despite the fairly good success of conventional distance measure in CBIR application, several distance metrics, such as the Manhattan Distance (MD), the Euclidean Distance (ED) and the Vector Cosine Angle Distance (VCAD) are proposed in the literature for measuring similarity between feature vectors. Several CBIR system were proposed using ED and MD.

Although, Minkowski distance is most widely used metric for measuring the similarity in CBIR systems, this measure fail to capture the true similarity/ dissimilarity measure in perceptual space. The use of advance similarity/dissimilarity measure like Kullback-Leibler Divergence (KLD), EMD etc., are shown to be more efficient in capturing the perceptual distance between two images.

The EMD is based on the transportation problem and recently, many methods have been proposed to improve the efficiency and accuracy of EMD. The quality of the EMD for image similarity has been demonstrated in several application scenarios: color, contour matching, texture, melodies, visual tracking, etc. Its high quality for image similarity search has been demonstrated in an extensive survey on distances for CBIR. To benefit from the EMD's high quality retrieval in these settings, efficient storage and query processing is crucial.

CBIR systems using relevance feedback mechanism: Generally, low level features such as color, texture, shape, corner, etc., are used to represent the approximate perceptual representation of an image, by using which similarity and dissimilarity of the images are computed. But this low level information is not sufficient to describe the semantic relation among different image regions, object and background and different object in the fore-ground as well as in the background. Moreover, overall perceptual meaning of an image depicting different events/incidence cannot be described using such low level image representation.

Jin *et al.* have proposed a feature re-weighting technique by using both the relevant and the irrelevant information, to obtain more effective results. Relevance feed-back is considered as a learning and classification process, using classifiers like Neural etworks, Support Vector Machine (SVM), Least Square SVM (LS-SVM/LSSVM), etc.

SVM-based relevance feedback is one of the most widely used approaches in the field of CBIR. Despite its success, it considers the positive and negative feedbacks equally which is not robust base since each sample has distinct properties. In addition, most of SVM based relevance feedback approaches do not consider unlabeled samples which may yield a weak classifier during the refinement process. Bian and Tao proposed a new SVM-based relevance feedback technique using a new type of learning, referred as the Biased Discriminative Euclidean Embedding (BDEE). Zhang *et al.* have also proposed another SVM-based relevance feedback scheme, namely the Biased Maximum Margin Analysis (BMMA) and Semi-supervised BMMA (Semi-BMMA). This utilizes the information of unlabeled samples and integrate the distinct properties of feedbacks. However, trained classifiers become less effective when the training samples are insufficient in number. To overcome such problems, active learning methods are also used.

A frequent adding of images to the CBIR system may result in degrading the performance of long-term learning relevance feedback methods. Additionally, the recorded feedbacks in such methods are often sparse. To take care of these problems, Rashedi *et al.* proposed a long term learning method by adopting the Case-Based Reasoning (CBR), which is called the Case-Based Long Term Learning (CB-LTL).

To consider the user preferences and subjectivity during the retrieval process, Lai and Chen proposed a user-oriented mechanism based on the Interactive Genetic Algorithm (IGA) in the CBIR domain. Another relevance feedback approach based on the genetic programming was proposed by Ferreira *et al.* which considered both relevant and irrelevant images marked by the user.

The aim of a CBIR algorithm is to determine the images that are related to the QI from the database. CBIR can retrieve images that are similar to the query input image using the ''query by example" technique which requires the user to input any description about the query image. The system of CBIR works mainly by extracting features from the query image, then searching for these extracted features. These extracted features are used to calculate feature vector for the query image, CBIR represents every image in the database with a vector, after inputting the QI, the CBIR system computes its feature vector then compares it with the vectors stored for every image in the database. CBIR system returns the images that are similar in features to the QI.

Feng et al. proposed an image descriptor (Global Correlation Descriptor) for texture and color feature extraction respectively so that they had the same influence on CBIR. Global Correlation Vector and Directional Global Correlation Vector were also proposed, they integrated the benefits of structure element correlation and statistics of histogram to describe texture and color features. Corel-10 K and Corel-5 K datasets were used for validation, and the recall and precision were used for the efficiency evaluation.

In Zeng a local structure descriptor is proposed for image retrieval. Local structure descriptor is created based on the local structures underlying colors; it has combined the color, shape and texture as a one unit for retrieval of images. In addition, they proposed an algorithm for feature extraction which is able to extract local structure histogram using local structure descriptor.

Madhavi et al. proposed an approach known as image retrieval using interactive genetic algorithm for calculating a high number of selective features then comparing of related images for these features. The approach was tested on a group of 10,000 general images to prove the efficiency of the proposed approach.

Ali et al. presented a CBIR approach using integration of Speeded-Up Robust Features (SURF) and Scale Invariant Feature Transform (SIFT). The representations of these local features are used for retrieval because SIFT is robust to rotation and scale change, and SURF is more robust to illumination changes. The integration of SURF and SIFT enhances the effectiveness of CBIR. The comparisons and evaluation were conducted on Corel-1500, Corel-2000, and Corel-1000.

One of the most commonly used meta-heuristics in optimization problems is the genetic algorithm. Genetic algorithm (GA) is a search algorithm which stimulates the heredity in the living things. GA is very effective in finding the optimum solution from the search space.

In order to enhance the performance of a meta-heuristic such as GA, a local search algorithm is needed to help the GA for exploiting the solution space rather than just concentrating on exploring the search space. One excellent local search is the great deluge algorithm. The great deluge algorithm (GDA) was presented by Dueck as a local search algorithm. The main idea of this algorithm came from the analogy that someone is climbing a hill and trying to move in any direction to find a way up for keeping his feet dry and the water level is raising through a great deluge. The great deluge algorithm when inserted in the genetic algorithm was an effective way to yield a good solution instead of using the genetic algorithm alone.

Based on the abovementioned revision and discussion, this work utilizes a memetic algorithm (MA) to find the images that has the highest similarity with the QI from a database. During the CBIR process every image in the database is indicated by chromosome, from the QI the color signature, shape and color texture are extracted and also from the chromosomes that were generated. The next step is calculating fitness function for every chromosome using similarity difference equation. After that MA processes like crossover, mutation, great deluge local search and selection of the highest fitness chromosome are applied on the chromosomes; the CBIR retrieves the most relevant images from the images database.

Automatic image retrieval has become an important research problem considering its usage in handling the gigabytes of unlabeled image data that are generated and stored digitally in huge repositories, containing visual information both on the web as well as in the network computing system. These images, stored as unstructured multimedia data in different databases spread all over the world, most of which can be accessed through the Internet.

This growth can be attributed to the ease with which users are able to produce and archive photographs with today's consumer electronic devices. There are good reasons to believe that the rate of this growth will increase in the future, forcing search engine companies such as Google, Bing and Flickr to devote vast computational resources to their image search engines. However, reliable textual information about these photographs is hardly available, making the task of building effective image retrieval systems even more challenging. Moreover, uniformity can be a major problem in manually labeled collections because a human annotator may overlook a relevant description of an image or might disagree with another person over the "correct" interpretation of that image.

To overcome these limitations, Content Based Image Retrieval (CBIR) was proposed in the early 1990s. In the recent past, Google has launched a new application, called "Google Goggles" for Google Android mobile phones1, which is a content-based search application and allows people to search for more information about a famous landmark or work of art simply by taking a photo of that object. CBIR systems create machine-interpretable descriptions of an image's physical characteristics such as color, texture, shape etc. These descriptions, known as extracted features, can then be compared by a measure of similarity. The similarity between a given query image and every image in the image archive is then computed by CBIR system, and finally ranks the images in the collection according to their degree of relevance to the user's query. Even after designing several compact and efficient features vector for indexing each image, still there remains a wide gap between actual human perceptions model with that of feature based model used for CBIR. This is mainly due to the fact that the design of feature vector is solely based on low level visual information (like color, texture, shape etc.) without taking into account the semantic information like spatial organization, context, events etc. To overcome this shortcoming and in trying to incorporate certain amount of visual perception characteristic in the feature vector design, people have proposed the relevance feedback mechanism in CBIR design with active participation of human observers.

The typical CBIR system with relevance feedback is shown in Fig.1.1, where the building blocks without the dotted line box describe the general CBIR system and the building blocks with the dotted line describe the CBIR system with relevance feedback model. Images are being generated at an ever-increasing rate by sources such as defence and civilian satellites, military reconnaissance and surveillance flights, fingerprinting and mugshot capturing devices, scientific experiments, biomedical imaging, and home entertainment systems. Application areas in which CBIR has a principal activity are numerous and diverse: art galleries and museum management, architectural and engineering design law enforcement and criminal investigation, interior design, trademark and copyright database management, remote sensing and management of earth resources, scientific database management, weather forecasting, retailing, fabric and fashion design, Medical Imaging and picture archiving and communication systems. With the recent interest in multimedia systems, CBIR has attracted the attention of researchers across several disciplines.

A Brief Review of CBIR Systems: One of the major building blocks of a CBIR system is the feature extraction block. In the feature extraction block, an image is represented by features which allow searching for images similar to a given image. A feature is defined to capture a certain visual property of an image. Color, texture, shape, etc. are the most widely used features in CBIR applications. Several CBIR algorithms have been developed using only single features. A single feature normally describes a specific aspect of the image content; therefore multiple visual features are necessary for the general purpose CBIR. Recent research work uses multiple visual features, which can improve the retrieval performance effectively. Various multiple visual feature extraction schemes have been used in the literature to find the low-dimensional salient and significant features, which can effectively be used to represent the underlying image's visual characteristics. The most commonly used features in designing CBIR system are color, texture, shape, and keypoint descriptor and, brief discussion about each of which will be presented in the following paragraph. Besides that, descriptions about some commercially available CBIR system will also be presented. Different color features in CBIR systems: The color signature of object in the foreground and also that of the background makes it as one of the important vision ques. Color is considered to be a robust visual feature because it is invariant to direction, size, rotation and shift. Point/pixel and block/group based are the two different color representation schemes. Pixel based color representation includes color moments and Color Co occurrence Matrix (CCM), where color histogram and color correlogram comes under block/group based representation schemes.

In general, color spaces are classified into linear color spaces and non-linear color spaces. The RGB color space is an additive color space based on three primary colors: red, green and blue. Secondary colors can be generated by using the primary colors. However, the RGB space is not very efficient in dealing with real-world images, thus it is avoided in most of image retrieval algorithms because it lacks the ability of measuring the perceptual similarity. Accordingly, the HSV color space is used instead of the RGB color space because the components of hue and saturation are very close to human visual perception. The HSV model has three constituent components *i.e.*, the "hue" which refers to the color, the "saturation" which refers to the "vibrancy" of the color, and the "value" which to refers the brightness of the color. As another color space, the YCbCr color space is divided into luminance (Y) and chrominance (Cb, Cr), while Cb and Cr denote the blue-yellow and red-green color difference, respectively. The L^*a^*b color space is also derived from the XYZ color space to achieve perceptual uniformity. As in YCbCr, L^*a^*b consists of one lightness dimension (L) and two chrominance dimensions (a^*, b^*) based on the color opponent process.

Color histogram is a popular color representation that has been used in many image retrieval systems. Its performance in characterizing global color content has been widely recognized. However, color histograms lacks the information about the spatial distribution of color; thus, other representations such as color correlogram and auto-correlogram have been proposed. These methods provide information about the changes of the spatial correlation of color pairs with the distance in an image, and they have shown better retrieval performance than color histograms. In addition, many algorithms have been proposed

1.2 BACKGROUND

In recent years, research in analysing, matching, classification and indexing, and retrieval of images from a large volume of image databases is one of the hottest topics in image processing. There are many reasons for this, first the retrieval problem has got great practical interest. For instance, while digital cameras make pictures it requires volume of space and large amounts of new imagery become available on the web every day. There is still a great lacking of effective tools for searching and manipulating visual contents. Second, it touches a significant number of unsolved challenging questions in image understanding, e.g. image similarity, segmentation of various shapes, and shape invariance, etc. In the present scenario, the information retrieval becomes complicated since it has heterogeneous types of information like imagery objects, text, sound, colour, etc. This type of information or data analysis is coined as Big data analytics. But, this research work concentrates on classification, indexing, and the retrieval of images.

The advances in computer vision systems and the arrival of the World Wide Web, the usage of the digital libraries and the access of the image data through on-line have got exponential growth in the past decade. Many areas such as medical, educational, traffic management, law enforcement, automatic target recognition, and geographic information systems effectively utilize these advances in vision technology. Handling images, that is, manipulating, storing, analysing, indexing, matching, retrieval, display, etc., is a very complicated when compared to that of text manipulation. Thus, it needs proper image database systems, which can support the aforesaid image manipulations. It is observed from the literature that, remarkable progress has been made in both theoretical research and system development. However, it is a challenging problem for the researchers in the area of visual data mining to design an automatic retrieval system, because real-world images usually contain complicated objects and colour information. Mainly there are two methods of image retrieval systems: content-based and region-based image retrieval.

Before going through a brief introduction of the content-based and region-based image retrieval systems, let us discuss the evolution of the image retrieval system.

It is illustrated from the literature that image retrieval concept was introduced in the year 1970. In the year 1970, a conference on Database Techniques for Pictorial Applications [Blast79] was conducted in Florence. Since then, the application potential of image management techniques has attracted the attention of researchers [Chan79, Chan80, Chan81, Chan88]. The techniques introduced at the outset were generally not based on visual features but on the textual annotation of images. In other words, images were first annotated with text and then searched using a text-based approach from traditional database management system. A comprehensive survey of early text-based image retrieval methods can be found in [Chan80, Tamu84].

Through text description, images can be organised by topical or semantic hierarchies to facilitate easy navigation and browsing, based on standard Boolean queries. However, since automatically generating descriptive text for a wide spectrum of images is not feasible, most text-based image retrieval system requires manual annotation of images. Obviously, annotating image manually is a cumbersome and expensive task for large image databases, and is often subjective, context-sensitive and incomplete. For example, Figure 1.1 illustrates the text-annotation based image retrieval system.

Tiger, Forest			
Flower Images			
Park, Tree Images			

Figure 1.1: Images with textual keywords annotated by different users at different times

Therefore, an efficient management of rapidly expanding visual information became an urgent problem. This need urged and induced the researchers to develop the new techniques for fast image retrieval systems, such as content-based image retrieval (CBIR) and region-based image retrieval (RBIR) systems.

In 1992, the National Science Foundation (NSF) of the United States (USA) organised a workshop on visual management systems to identify new directions in image database management systems. Researchers from the communities of computer vision, database management, human-computer interface, and information retrieval were attracted to this field. The content-based image retrieval technique has attracted the attention of many researchers for over a decade. In this system, the researchers concentrated on developing low-level global visual features, such as colour properties, shape, texture, and spatial relationship and orientation, which are used as a query for the retrieval process [Huan97, Stri95, Pent94, Chio00]. The colour histogram, colour coherence vector, colour correlogram, and colour moments are the commonly used colour descriptors.

The colour moments have been successfully used in many retrieval systems, especially when the image contains just the object. The first order, mean; the second order, variance; the third order, skewness; and the colour moments have been provided to be efficient and effective in representing colour distributions of images [Stic95].

The colour histogram serves as an effective representation of the colour content of an image if the colour pattern is uniquely compared with the rest of the data set. The colour histogram is easy to compute and effective in characterising both global and local distribution of colours in an image. It is robust to translation and rotation about the view axis and changes slowly with the scale, occlusion and viewing angle.

A colour coherence vector (CCV) stores the number of coherent versus incoherent pixels with each colour. By separating coherent pixels from incoherent pixels, CCV's provide finer distinctions than colour histograms. Due to its additional spatial information, the CCV provides better retrieval results than the colour histogram especially for those images which have either mostly uniform colour or mostly texture regions in addition for both colour histogram and colour coherence vector representation. The HSV colour space provides better results than the CIE L*u*v and CIE L*a*b* space.

The colour correlogram characterizes not only the colour distributions of pixels, but also the spatial correlation of pairs of colours. The first and the second dimension of the three-dimensional histogram are the colours of any pixel pair and the third dimension is their spatial distance.

Colour Feature: Colour is the most extensively used visual content for image retrieval [Ioka89, Huan97, Huan99]. It is three-dimensional values, which makes its discrimination potentially superior to the single dimensional gray values of images. The colour space must be determined first, before selecting an appropriate colour description. Each pixel of the image can be denoted represented as a point in a 3D colour space. The one of the desirable characteristics of an appropriate colour space for image retrieval is its uniformity. Uniformity means that two colour pairs that are equal in similarity distance in colour space are perceived as equal by viewers. RGB (red, green, blue) colour component space is widely used colour space for image display, which is called additive primitives, since a colour in RGB space is produced by adding them together. The CMY colour component space is widely used for printing, which is called as subtractive primaries, since a colour in CMY space is produced through light absorption. The HSV (Hue, Saturation, and Value) colour component space is widely used in computer graphics and is a more intuitive way of describing colour. The HSV colour space is commonly used in the literature and is more intuitive to human visual system [Kim96, Kark03]. In the HSV colour space, the achromatic component is decoupled from chromatic component (hue and saturation). Furthermore, it is explored that classification performance of HSV is higher than the RGB colour space [Chen07]. This background reinforces the idea to propose a retrieval system on HSV colour space.

Shape Feature: Shape features contain potential information, which is useful for image retrieval [Gonz09] because human can recognize objects solely from the shapes or structures of an image. The efficient shape descriptors must present some essential properties [Zhan04] such as invariant to translation, rotation, and scaling, and robust to noise and compact representation. The shape based techniques are broadly categorized into two categories: region based and boundary based techniques; each category fall into global and structural approaches and further they are classified into spatial domain and transformed domain techniques [Pena12].

In the literature, several approaches have been proposed for region based shape representation and description, which includes Legendre moment [Teag80], morphology description [Hara87], Zernike moment [Khot90], convex hell [Sonk93], shape decomposition [Sann94], grid shape descriptor [Chak00], pseudo Zernike moment [Kan02], Fourier-Mellin moment [Kan02], shape context [Belo02], MPEG-7's region-based shape derived from Zernike moments [Ciep01, Manj02]. On the same direction, a number of techniques have been proposed by various researchers [Anda10, Mich11] for image retrieval. However, the region based shape representation may not be easy and reliable, since there is no generalized accurate automatic scheme for region based approach [Müll04, Pena12]. For example, a region based technique may be appropriate for the medical images. But the same technique may not be appropriate for the images in other domains. Even the region based technique is suitable for one class of medical images, may not be suitable for another class of medical images.

Since human beings recognize shapes mainly by their boundary features and in many shape applications, the shape contour is the only interest, boundary based methods are more familiar than the region based methods [Liu07]. For instance, Freeman [Free78] proposes a chain code method and it describes an object by a sequence of unit-size line segments with a given orientation; the chain code histogram (CCH) is described in [Iiva96] for object recognition; the simple global contour descriptors such as area, eccentricity, circularity, bending energy, major axis orientation, convexity, ratio of principle axis, elliptic variance and circular variance are discussed in [Yong74, Peur97]; the shape signatures namely centroidal profile, cumulative angle, complex coordinates, tangent angle, curvature, chord-length, etc. are reported in [Otte91, Zhan02]; boundary moments [Sonk93, Gonz09]; elastic matching [Del97]; scale space method [Mokh86, Manj02, Voge06] and stochastic model based approaches [He91, Seki92] are proposed in the literature for shape based image retrieval. Consequently, Groskey et al. [Gros92] suggested Polygon decomposition in which shape boundary is broken down into line segments by polygon approximation and is further enhanced in [Berr00]; shape invariants [Huan98] namely cross-ratio, length ratio, distance ratio, angle and triangle; trace and invariants from coplanar points [Sonk93]; determinants; Eigen values [Squi00]; etc. are reported in the literature. In the same direction, a number of research efforts [Quel10, Wang11, Coll12] have been taken by various researchers. However, Zhang and Lu [Zhan04] reported that spatial domain based contour techniques are affected by noise sensitivity problem, some of them are not suitable to be a standalone shape descriptors, complex in implementation and matching, failure to capture global shape features and high computation cost.

In order to overcome the shortcomings, the researchers used spectral domain based approaches, such as Fourier descriptor [Otte91, Arbt90] and wavelet descriptor [Ohm00]. Though the wavelet descriptor outperforms the Fourier descriptor, the increase of spatial resolution will certainly sacrifice frequency resolution and matching of wavelet representation is complex, which makes it impractical for online shape retrieval.

Shape features of objects or regions have been used in many content-based image retrieval systems [Gros90, Jaga91, Tego94]. The shape description is categorized into *boundary-based* and *region-based* systems. This type of techniques segregate the various regions into different shapes and extract the features in the shapes, and compare the features region-wise.

Texture: Texture feature is a metric to measure the surface of an image, which reflects the relationship among the pixels in local area, and also reflects the changes of the image space at gray-level. There are different methods for extracting texture features, which differ in the way the spatial relationship between the image pixels are observed.

The texture features are computed at specified positions relative to each other in the image from the statistical distribution of observed combinations of intensities. Statistics are classified into first order and second order statistics based on number of intensity points (pixels) in each combination. Statistical-based methods explain the grey-level relationship between the pixels through either first order (single pixels) statistics of histograms that do not take into consideration neighbourhood pixel interactions, or second order (grey-level) statistics that describes the relationship between the pixels through displacement distance and orientation. Model-based methods rely upon capturing the fundamental qualities of the studied texture through constructing an image model having certain parameters. Foremost applications of Texture analysis, such as classification, segmentation, synthesis and compression are briefly discussed below [Tuce93].

Texture is an important characteristic for the analysis of many types of images, such as classification, segmentation, synthesis, restoration, compression, and image retrieval are briefly discussed below [Tuce93]. It can be seen in all the images from multispectral scanner images get from aircraft or satellite platforms to microscopic images of cell cultures or tissue samples. Despites its importance and ubiquity in an image data, a formal approach or precise definition of texture does not exist. Texture representation methods can be classified into two categories: *structural* and *statistical*.

Structured Approach

Structural models of texture are based on the visual perception that textures are made up of primitives which appear in near regular repetitive spatial arrangements. To describe the texture, we must describe the primitives and the placement rules.

Statistical Approach

In the context of image processing, statistical based approach plays a significant role, where textures are modeled based on the concept of the joint probability distributions or the conditional probability density functions of the arrangement of the texture surface.

The structural method, including morphological operator and adjacency graph, describe texture by identifying structural primitives and their placement rules. They tend to be most effectiveness when applied to textures that are very regular.

Statistical methods including *Fourier power spectra, co-occurrence matrices, shift-invarient principal component analysis, Tamura features, Wold decomposition, Markov random field,* and *multi-resolution filtering techniques* such as *Gabor* and *Wavelet transform*, characterise texture by a number of texture representations [Voor88, Tamu78, Mao92, Manj96, Kank94, Liu96], which have been used frequently and proved to be effective in content-based image retrieval systems.

Spatial relationship: Regions or objects with similar colour and texture properties can be easily distinguished by imposing spatial constraints. The most widely used representation of spatial relationship is the 2D strings [Chan87]. In addition to the 2D-strings, spatial quad-tree [Same84] and symbolic images [Gudi95] are also used for spatial information representation. However, searching images based on spatial relationship of regions remains a difficult research problem in content-based image retrieval because reliable segmentation of objects or regions is often not feasible.

These features are used to represent and index images. Jing *et al.* [Jing04] suggested that a single signature computed for the entire image cannot sufficiently capture the important features of individual objects and there is a gap between the visual features and semantic concepts of images. To overcome this problem, the region-based system is developed [Jing04, Jun03, Belo02, Jing01, Deng99], which represent the focus of the user's perceptions of the image contents. In this method, the entire image is classified / segmented [Ing01, Smit99, Wang01, Kimu91, Ho94, Chio00] into various regions according to the objects / structures present in the image. Then the region-to-region comparison is made to measure the similarity between two images [Pent94, Simt99, Wang01]. In this system, the user has to provide one or several regions from the query image to start a query session. Automatic and precise extraction of image objects is still beyond the ability of the retrieval system available with computer vision [Wang01]. Therefore, the above system tends to partition one object into several regions; none of them is representative of the semantic object. Edge oriented segmentation algorithms are available for both region-based and content-based retrieval systems. This type of techniques use features of local edges, and the edges are classified based on two factors such as orientation and correlation between neighbouring edges [Theo05]. Hence, it contains information of continuous edges and lines of images, and describes major shape characteristics of images. The main drawback of the system is to determine which region is to be used as feedback query image example for retrieval [Jing04]. In this type of systems, when either the target image or the query image is rotated with a particular angle, the corresponding regions of both the images may not match exactly. So, it is not robust for the same image with different angles.

Su, *et al*. [Su03] suggested that the content-based retrieval system yields results with low accuracy and slow response time, because there is a big research gap between semantic concepts and low-level image features. A concept, relevance feedback is used to bridge the gap [Su03, Cox00, Rui99]. The degree of relevance (to the query) of each of the *n* positive feedback images is calculated by the user at each of the feedback iteration. Since, the positive feedback images are choosen by the user with the use of iterative technique, this technique demands computational complexity. Minka and Picard [Mink97] proposed the Four Eyes system, which also has two disadvantages: (i) it uses the region-to-region similarity measure; (ii) the re-clustering of all the features when a new image is added. Thus it is not very scalable [Jing04]. Jing *et al.* [Jing04] proposed a system with the following features, but it requires high computational efforts because, it computes probabilistic interpretation and it has been used in region matching; region codebook is used; the SVM based classifier and clustering techniques are employed. In addition to all these things, it requires the positive and negative query image examples. Again here arises the problem of how to select the negative and positive image examples to refine the query. To avoid this problem, many researchers [Jing01, Wang01, Mink97, Gree00, Gree01, Jing02] have taken efforts to integrate the information from all the regions in an image and then the image-to-image similarity measure (integrated information) is used to compares the images. For instance, SIMPLIcity system [Wang01] uses an integrated region matching as the similarity measure. In summary, the review highlights that the region-based technique again tends to the concept of the content-based retrieval by using the integrated information of the several regions. The region-based technique also requires high computational efforts.

It is observed from the literature that statistical methods play a noteworthy role in the domain of computer vision, pattern recognition, and machine learning and especially in image mining that play a good role.

Aksoy, et al. [Akso01] proposes a probabilistic approach for image retrieval, which describes two likelihood-based similarity measures that compute the likelihood query and target images are being similar or dissimilar. The likelihood values are derived from Bayesian classifier. Barnard et al. [Barn03] presented a probability-based similarity measure that combines the information provided by text and the visual information provided by image features. The oharatos, *et al.* [Theo05] proposed a system, based on a multivariate non-parametric test namely, Wald-Wolfowitz test (WW-test), and graph theoretic framework of minimal-spanning-tree (MST). Chen et al. [Chen06] introduce an efficient indexing and searching method for image retrieval from large databases using the principal axis analysis is presented. In which the image objects are represented by high-dimensional feature vectors, which are obtained by scanning the segmented regions in a top-to-bottom and left-to-right fashion and characterizing these regions as their mean colours and shape parameters. Ozden and Polat [Ozde07] proposes a nonparametric based method for segmenting colour images and compares region-wise, then retrieves the similar images. It uses median energy, k-means algorithm, and mean-shift algorithm as features. Yang and Xiao [Yang08] propose a statistical features based method, which uses wavelet transform, based on energy measure, mean, variance and gray-level co-occurrence matrix of the values of wavelet coefficients. Kekre, et al. [Kekr11] propose a method, which reduces the two-dimensional data to one-dimensional using principal component analysis and it connects the edges to form a boundary of the shapes. It make use of the DCT transform to design the sectors required for the search and retrieval of the images from a database. Igbal et al. [Igba12] introduce a system for biometric security, which uses three algorithms such as colour histogram, Gabor filter and moment invariant that are controlled by the fuzzy heuristics. There are some drawbacks in he method introduced in [Theo05]. They are as follows:

(ii) Construction of the MST demands computational overhead.

(iii) Based on the sample identities of the points, running length of each sample identical identities is computed and then the WW-test is used to identify whether the query and target images are the same.

The pixel values in the images are quantized, so that the parametric test can be applied straight without converting the content of the image as qualitative values that are either 0 or 1 as in [Theo05]. By applying the parametric test straight, the additional computational headache can be avoided. The non-parametric tests do not yield good results compared to the parametric tests.

The distance measures play a significant role in matching and retrieving images, especially in the CBIR systems. The distance measures can be categorized into pairwise (point by point comparison) approach and distributional approach (massive comparison). The former is precise and simple, but it is not robust for rotation and scaling, while the latter is robust, and at the same time it is effective and efficient. Moreover, in the case of latter, the user can match and retrieve only the required number of images by fixing significance level for the test statistic at a particular level. This is not possible in the case of former, since there is no such option; thus, the user has to select same or similar images from the list of retrieved images.

Though a number of works have been developed based on the statistical distributional approaches and parametric tests of hypothesis, most of them perform moderately, since there is no guarantee that all the images are distributed as lonely and identical to Gaussian random process. The statistical parametric tests can be applied to an image, if it is distributed to Gaussian process. Otherwise, it does not lead to a good result. In general, the parametric tests can be used if the data are quantitative and are distributed as independent and identical to Gaussian process.

The Bhattacharyya distance (BD) measure is appropriate for feature extraction. Many researchers have used the BD [Kail67, Ray89, Choi03] and Kullback-Liebler distance (KLD) measures in control theory and signal processing for feature extraction and comparing the distance between two distributions. The work proposed in [Ali66, Csis67] reports that the divergence, 'div', between any two probability distributions, P1 and P2, should satisfy the following properties: div(P_1,P_2) ≥ 0, and div(P_1,P_2) = 0 if and only if $P_1 = P_2$. The latter reveals that the two probability distributions are equal if there is no divergence (distance) between them and vice versa. In the case of Bhattacharyya, the probabilities of two distributions are assumed to be equal, i.e. $P_1 = P_2 = 1/2$ [Fuku90]. This means that both distributions have equal probabilities, with optimum value1/ 2. But, in the case of real-life images, there is no such assurance. Thus, in the context of image retrieval, the Bhattacharyya distance metric yields moderate results than other existing metrics.

As suggested in [Choi03], the BD measure is superior to the KLD measure in terms of time complexity. There are some difficulties in using the BD measures, i.e. the BD measure can be employed to extract features, and compare two distributions only if they follow Gaussian properties; otherwise, it cannot be applied. Zhang, et al. [Zhan11] suggest that there are some obstacles on assuming the images as Gaussian process. Abou-Moustafa, et al. [Mous12] report that the BD and KLD measures do not satisfy all metric axioms necessary for many algorithms. Thus, they propose a modification on the KLD and the BD for multivariate Gaussian densities; then it transforms the two measures into distance metrics. Even after the modification, they do not yield better results. The Chernoff distance (CD) measure overcomes the difficulties, since it adjusts itself and strictly follows the Gaussian properties. The BD is a special case of the CD measure, and also the CD measure becomes Mahalanobis distance (MD) while the covariance matrices of the two distributions are same (for more details the readers can refer to APPENDIX). The BD [Fuku90] and KLD are not metrics [Cove91], since they violate at least one of the distance axioms. Sinanovic and Johnson [Sina] analyse the distance measures - KLD, CD, and BD - and suggest that the CD is better than the BD. Hence, it is believed that the CD measure will lead to better results than the KLD, BD, and MD measures. Kokare, et al. [Koka03] perform a comparison of nine similarity measures such as Manhattan, Weighted-Mean-Variance, Euclidean, Chebychev, Mahalanobis, Canberra, Bray-Curtis, Squared-Chord, and Squared Chi-square distances, and report that the Canberra and Bray-Curtis distance measures give better results than the Euclidean and Mahalanobis distance measures. But, they consider only texture images in the experiment, and also do not discuss the robustness for the rotation, scaling, and noise. In [Koka03], since most of the distance measures are based on the point processing except Mahalanobis and Weighted-Mean-Variance distances, they do not yield better results for rotated and scaled images. In the case of MD, if we put $M_q = M_t = M$ in Eq. (A.1) of the APPENDIX, then the MD becomes zero. It means that there is no distance between the two distributions, i.e. the two distributions are same. Since the Mahalanobis distance metric fully depends on the mean value of the distributions, the decision taken based on the distance can lead to wrong results. Generally, though the mean vectors of the two distributions are equal, there is no constraint that the covariance matrices are to be same. In such case, it is not possible for the two distributions to be same. This is the main drawback of the MD measure. Thus, it gives a poor results when compared to that of the others as reported in [Koka03].

Furthermore, bivariate statistical tests of hypothesis, such as F-ratio and Welch's test statistic are adopted. First, the input query image is segmented into various regions according to its structure. If it is a gray-scale, which is considered as it is; otherwise, it is assumed that the image is colour, and it is transformed to HSV colour model. The V represents the intensity values of the pixels, and also it represents the gray-scale. The test statistic expressed in equation (2), i.e. F-ratio test, tests the equality of the variances of the query and target images region-wise. If the variances pass the test, then it is proceeded to perform the equality of mean values of both images region-wise, i.e. Welch's test is applied. If the variances and mean values pass the two tests at a particular significant level, namely according to users' suit, it is inferred that the two images are same or similar; otherwise, it is concluded that the two images are not similar. This is discussed in detailed in Chapter 3.

Motivation: The work proposed in [Tai05, Kato06, and Sala[11] reports that the segmented homogeneous regions in a structured image are distributed to Gaussian random process or the image is assumed to be Gaussian random process. The Orthogonal polynomial methods in [Kris13] yields moderate results to the noisy images compared to that of other images, because OP includes Haar Wavelet transform which is not tolerable for noise. It is also time consuming, since it involves the computation of model coefficients, and genetic algorithm is used to find optimized weight for each feature.

These lead to the computational complexity of the orthogonal polynomial method.

In [Suma12], Kullback-Liebler distance is used with the texture features extracted from query and target images. This dependents fully on generalised Gaussian density features.

Sumana, et. al. have applied this method to the texture images only, not experimented on all type of images.

In the case of Bhattacharyya distance [Yang13] the terms P_q and P_t are fixed to 1/2, whereupon it does not yield better results than the other existing methods because nature -- the structure and content -- of the images varies from image to image; so they can have an effect on P_q and P_t values. Thus, it is not rational to fix P_q to 1/2 in the context of automated image retrieval or analysis. As the BD is a special case of the CD, it leads to moderate results for all types of images while compared to the CD. This method uses only texture and semi-structure images.

The Mahalanobis distance method proposed in [Hoi10], is a special case of the Chernoff distance. The reasons discussed above motivated us to develop the proposed method.

In this research work, an attempt is made to test whether texture images are distributed to either Gaussian process or mixed or other than the Gaussian process or distribution free. In order to examine that the texture images are distributed to Gaussian process or others, a manifold texture images are included in the test. The outcome of the test reveals that most of the texture images, either natural or artificial, are not distributed as independent and identical to Gaussian process.

For a sample, due to space constraint, only two of the number of images considered for the experiment are presented in this thesis, and the results obtained are shown in Figure 4. The results reveal that the images presented in Figure 4 are not distributed to Gaussian process, because they do not follow the symmetric property of the Gaussian distribution, i.e. the image presented in Figure 4(a) is skewed to left tail, and the image presented in Figure 4(b) is skewed to right tail. In such a case, the BD measure is not appropriate; so it give moderate results. In this context the CD measure can be adopted, since it adapts itself to the nature of the images (either the image is distributed to Gaussian or mixed or other than the Gaussian or even distribution free), and so it yields better results than the BD measure. In this research work, it is believed that in some cases a segmented region of the image does not follow the Gaussian process because entire or almost the intensity values of all the pixels can be same. For instance, let us consider the cheek region of the lady's head image presented in Figure 8. The pixel intensity values in the cheek might be distributed to uniform process (uniformly distributed - follows uniform distribution), since almost all the pixel intensity values are same in the region. This motivated us to develop the proposed research work. The obtained results are presented in section 5, and the results show that the CD measure outperforms the OP method, KLD, BD and MD measures. The proposed test statistic is discussed in detailed in Chapter 2.

Furthermore, bivariate statistical tests of hypothesis, such as F-ratio and Welch's test statistic are adopted. First, the input query image is segmented into various regions according to its structure. If it is a gray-scale, which is considered as it is; otherwise, it is assumed that the image is colour, and it is transformed to HSV colour model. The V represents the intensity values of the pixels, and also it represents the gray-scale. The test statistic expressed in equation (2), i.e. F-ratio test, tests the equality of the variances of the query and target images region-wise. If the variances pass the test, then it is proceeded to perform the equality of mean values of both images region-wise, i.e. Welch's test is applied. If the variances and mean values pass the two tests at a significant level, namely according to users' suit, it is inferred that the two images are same or similar; otherwise, it is concluded that the two images are not similar. This is discussed in detailed in Chapter 3.

Overview of the Proposed Method

First, the proposed method performs a pre-process on the input query image, viz. removes outliers or noise on the input query image, by employing the outlier method, which removes the noises in the images, discussed in section 2.1. Then the query image is examined to know whether it is texture or structure. If the query image is a structure, then it is segmented into various regions according to its nature, and the regions are counted; if the number of regions in the query and target images match, then it is proceeded to the test statistic; otherwise, it is inferred that the two images are different. If the query image is texture, then it is considered as for the experiment. The test statistic discussed in section 2.2 is applied on the noise removed query image. The test statistic between the query and target images is tested, and if the distance is minimal, then the associative probability is computed on the same query image. Position vectors are computed based on the probability values. The orthogonality test is performed on the position vectors of the query and target images. If the test statistic and the angle between the two images are minimal, then it is inferred that the two images are same or similar. The same or similar images are marked and indexed in ascending order.

The main objective of this research work is to obtain a common framework for supporting automatic colour image retrieval system, which is robust for scaling, rotation, and noise. The proposed system extracts features of the RGB colour and relationship among the pixel values for fast retrieval with high precision, and to make the framework more general, which is employed for retrieving both textured and untextured images.

Chapters 2 and 3 discuss the statistical tests of hypothesis such as multivariate parametric and bivariate parametric test statistics. The test statistic, such as F-ratio, Welch's test statistic, Chernoff distance measure and, cosine-direction-based orthogonality test are employed to match and retrieve the images.

1.3 TEST STATISTIC FOR IMAGE RETRIEVAL

The statistical methods, such as bivariate parametric and multivariate parametric statistical tests of hypotheses are employed to extract the features, and the features are compared to match the query and target images. The matched images are indexed according to the results obtained from the statistical tests. Furthermore, to emphasis the similarity of the images the Bhattacharyya distance is used to measure the divergence between the query and target images.

In the proposed technique, first, the relationships among the pixel within the image and between the images are tested, if they pass the test then it proceeds to test the spectrum of energy between the two images; otherwise, the test is dropped or cancelled. Here, either the query image or the target image is treated as sample, and the other is treated as population. If the existence of the relationship among the pixels within the image and between the images, and the spectrum of energy between the images are confirmed, then it can be concluded that the two images are same; otherwise, it is assumed that they differ.

Generally, when capturing an image through camera (digital or analog) or scanning through scanner, there are many possibilities to add noise with the image. The addition of noise is a random process, which is independently and identically distributed to Gaussian random process. Let X be a random variable that represents the intensity value with additive noise of a pixel at location (k, l) in a colour image. The pixel $X(k, l) \in \Re^3$ is a linear combination of three colours, namely red, green, and blue, i.e. $X(k, l)=[r(k, l), g(k, l), b(k, l)]^T$, where T represents the transformation of the vector.

1.4 Bi-variate PARAMETRIC STATISTICAL ANALYSIS FOR IMAGE MATCHING

Furthermore, bivariate statistical tests of hypothesis, such as F-ratio and Welch's test statistic are adopted. First, the input query image is segmented into various regions according to its structure. If it is a gray-scale, which is considered as it is; otherwise, it is assumed that the image is colour, and it is transformed to HSV colour model. The V represents the intensity values of the pixels, and also it represents the gray-scale. The test statistic expressed in equation (2), i.e. F-ratio test, tests the equality of the variances of the query and target images region-wise. If the variances pass the test, then it is proceeded to perform the equality of mean values of both images region-wise, i.e. Welch's test is applied. If the variances and mean values pass the two tests at a particular significant level, namely according to users' suit, it is inferred that the two images are same or similar; otherwise, it is concluded that the two images are not similar. This is discussed in detailed in Chapter 3.

To perform the above tests, let us assume that *X* be a random variable that represents the intensity value with additive noise of a pixel at location (*k, l*) in a colour image. Thus, an image is assumed to be Gaussian Markov Random field [Kris07, Seet07, Seet [11]. To emphasis, experimentally, the intensity values of the natural images are distributed to Gaussian process or mixture of Gaussian process the tiger images given in Figure 1.2 are considered and the intensity values of the colour pixels are plotted in a line graph and the obtained graphical representations are presented in Figures 1.2 and 1.3. The mean spectrum of energy of intensity values of each colour with the pixels in the image is represented by μ, and the variation is denoted by σ^2. The normal density function of X (k, l) for each colour is given by,

$$\frac{1}{\sigma\sqrt{2\Pi}} \exp\left(-(x-\mu)^2/2\sigma^2\right), \; -\infty < x, \mu < \infty, \sigma > 0 \qquad \ldots (1.1)$$

The density function in equation (1.1) can be denoted as,

$N(x/\mu, \sigma^2)$ and the distribution law as $N(\mu, \sigma^2)$.

The proposed technique is applied on various types of images, and proved that it is robust for scaling, rotated, and some parts missed images. The detailed discussion and the experimental results are presented in Chapter 2.

Figure 1.2: Similar Tiger Images with same sizes - row 1: actual image with size 75×96; row 2: actual images with size 96×128; row 3: images rotated with 90 degrees; row 4: images rotated with 180 degrees

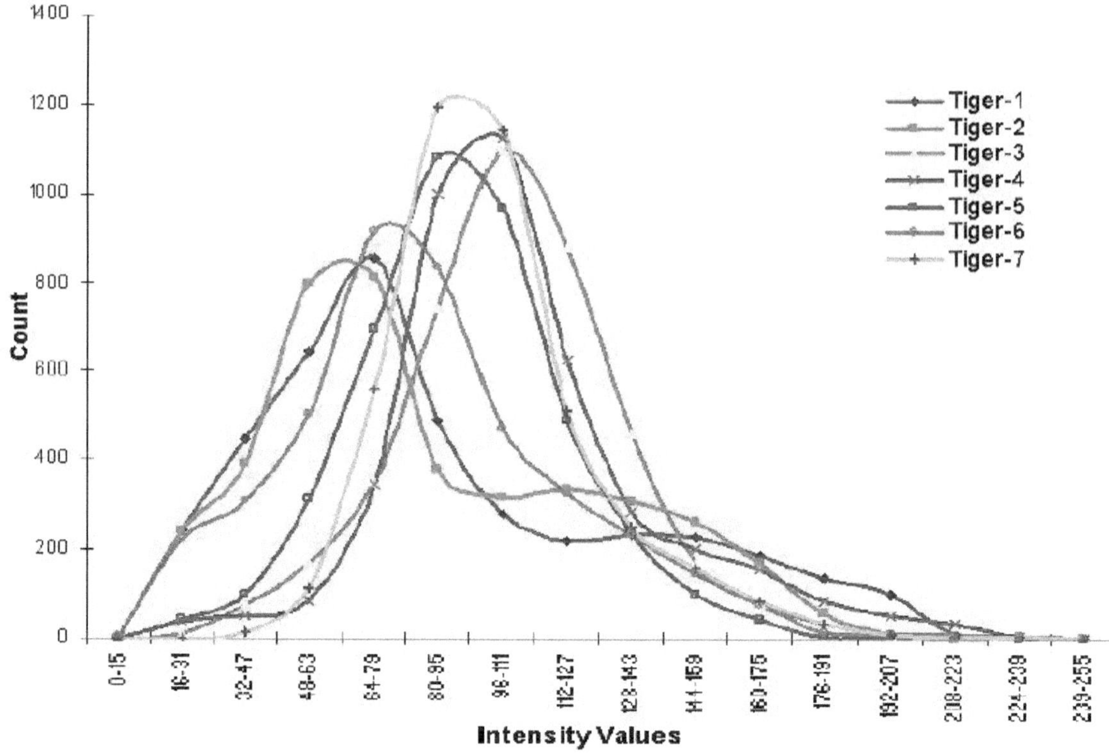

Figure 1.3: Line-Graph: Tiger images shown in row 2 of the Figure 1.2

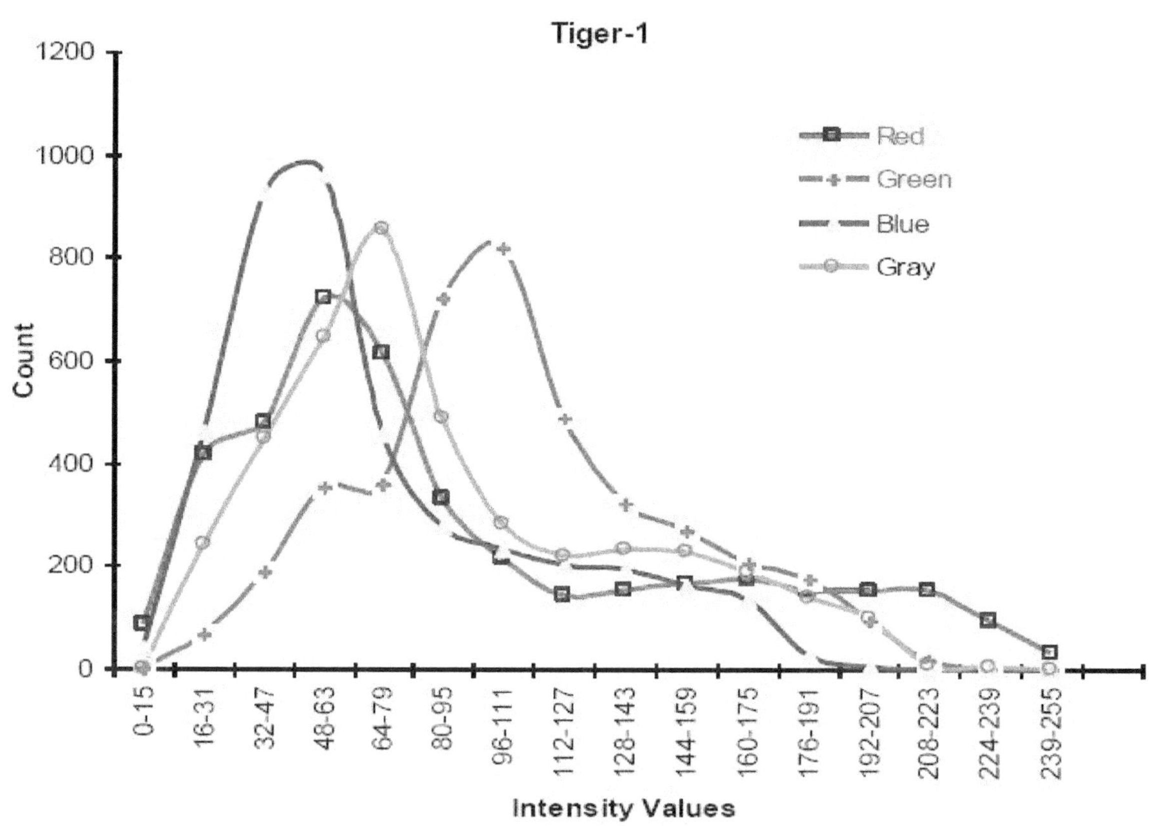

Figure 1.4: Tiger 1 - Line graph for individual colours

1.5 MULTIVARIATE PARAMETRIC STATISTICAL ANALYSIS FOR IMAGE MATCHING

Furthermore, to measure the similarity between the query and target images, the colour and texture features such as relationships among the pixels within and between the images, and the spectrum of energy are considered together and tested using multivariate statistical tests. To perform this, multivariate statistical tests of hypothesis such as test for equality of covariance matrices and test for equality of mean vectors are considered.

The multivariate normal density function of $X(k, l)$ is given by

$$\frac{1}{\left(\sqrt{2\Pi}\right)^3} \left|\Sigma\right| \exp(^{-1}2(x-\mu)^T\Sigma\text{-}1(x-\mu) \qquad \text{... (1.2)}$$

The density function mentioned in equation (1.2) can be denoted as $n(x/\mu,\Sigma)$ and the distribution law as $N(\mu,\Sigma)$. The i-the diagonal element, σ_{ii}, of the covariance matrix represents variance of the ith component of $X(k, l)$. The mean spectrum of energy of the pixels in the image is represented in the vector form as given in equation (1.3).

$$\mu=E(X)=E\begin{bmatrix} x_r \\ x_g \\ x_b \end{bmatrix} = \begin{bmatrix} \mu_r \\ \mu_g \\ \mu_b \end{bmatrix} \qquad \text{... (1.3)}$$

and the covariance matrix is,

$$\Sigma=\begin{bmatrix} \sigma_{rr} & \sigma_{rg}\rho & \sigma_{rb}\rho \\ \sigma_{gr}\rho & \sigma_{gg}\rho & \sigma_{gb}\rho \\ \sigma_{br}\rho & \sigma_{bg}\rho & \sigma_{bb}\rho \end{bmatrix} = \begin{bmatrix} \sigma_r^2 & \sigma_{rg}\rho & \sigma_{rb}\rho \\ \sigma_{gr}\rho & \sigma_g^2 & \sigma_{gb}\rho \\ \sigma_{br}\rho & \sigma_{bg}\rho & \sigma_b^2 \end{bmatrix} \qquad \text{... (1.4)}$$

where, σ_r^2, σ_g^2, and σ_b^2 are the variances of intensity values with red, green, and blue colours respectively, and ρ represents the correlation or interaction between the corresponding colour pixels. The covariance matrix Σ is symmetric and positive definite. The proposed method is employed for different types of images, and proved that it is robust for scaling, rotation, and some parts missed images. The detailed discussion and the experimental results are presented in Chapter 3.

1.6 IMAGE RETRIEVAL BASED ON ORTHOGONALITY AND DISTANCE MEASURES

In general, feature extraction can be considered as a process of transforming high dimensional data into a low dimensional feature space based on an optimization criterion. In other words, reducing dimensionality without a serious loss of class separability is the key to feature extraction. Canonical Correlation Analysis (CCA) is one of the most well-known examples of feature extraction [Rich93]. The CCA introduces a within-class scatter matrix, Σ_W and a between-class scatter matrix, Σ_b, to maximize a separation criterion is known as the Fisher criterion:

$$J = tr\left(\Sigma_W^{-1} \Sigma_b\right) \qquad \text{... (1.5)}$$

Unfortunately, the criterion of equation (1.5) is not directly related to the classification error which has been the ultimate measure of feature effectiveness for classification in the transformed space, although there has been an attempt to connect the criterion to the Bayes Error using a pair-wise weighting function for multi-class problems [Loog01]. For pattern classification, it may be optimal to use the minimum achievable error, the Bayes error, as a criterion [Fugu90].

However, the Bayes error cannot be easily expressed in an analytical form except in special cases. Instead, an estimate of the Bayes error is often used as a criterion. Buturovi proposed to use the *k-NN* estimate of Bayes error in the transformed space as an optimization criterion [Butu94]. Here, the Bayes error is approximated by upper and lower error bounds for the appropriate range of *k*, and then minimized using the simplex algorithm in the space spanned by transformation matrix coefficients. Apparently, the performance of this method depends on *k*. However, determining an optimal value of *k* is not an easy problem. Recently, it has been reported that an accurate estimation of classification error is possible using the Bhattacharyya distance [Lee00]. Thus, it is proposed to approximate the classification error using the error estimation equation based on the Bhattacharyya distance as an optimization criterion assuming normal distributions. A benefit of this approach is that the number of features necessary for classification without serious information loss can be predicted. The proposed feature extraction method is examined for different kinds of images, and proved that it is robust for scaling, rotation, and some parts missed images. The detailed discussion and the experimental results are presented in Chapter 4.

The rest of the thesis is organized as follows. Matching the similarity of images and retrieval using non-parametric bivariate statistical tests of hypotheses is discussed in Chapter 2. Image matching, indexing and retrieval based on multivariate statistical tests of hypotheses are discussed in Chapter 3.

Chapter 4 describes the feature extraction based on orthogonal and distance based measures such as Bhattacharyya distance, and the measure of performance of the proposed techniques such as Recall and Precision method. The discussion and conclusion of the thesis and recommendations for further research work are presented in Chapter 5.

CHAPTER 2

BIVARIATE PARAMETRIC STATISTICAL TESTS OF HYPOTHESES FOR MATCHING SIMILARITY OF IMAGES

2.1 INTRODUCTION

Representation is fundamental in both biological and computational vision system [Jenk97]. An effective, efficient and suitable representation is the key starting point for building image processing and computer vision system. In many ways, the success or failure of an algorithm depends greatly on an appropriately designed representation. In the computer vision community, it is a common practice to classify representation schemes as low-level, intermediate-level and high-level. Low-level deals with pixel level features, high-level deals with abstract concepts and intermediate-level deals with something in between. Whilst low-level vision is fairly well studied and we have a good understanding at this level, middle and high level concepts are very difficult to grasp, certainly extremely difficult to represent using computer bits. In the signal processing community, an image can be represented in the time/spatial domain and in the frequency/spectral domain. Both time domain and frequency domain analysis technologies are very well developed [Akan92, Robe87]. A signal/image can be represented as time sequence or transform coefficients of various types - Fourier, Wavelet, Gabor, KLT, etc. These coefficients often provide a convenient way to interpret and exploit the physical properties of the original signal. Exploiting well-established signal and analysis technology to represent and interpret vision concepts could be a fertile area for making progress. The human vision system is extremely sophisticated and more powerful. The human vision theories could provide guidance for building practical engineering solution to vision tasks [Mojs00].

Content-based image and vision indexing and retrieval have been a popular research subject in many fields related to computer science for over a decade. Of all the challenging issues, associated tasks with the indexing and retrieval tasks are probably most difficult to achieve. The difficulties can be explained from a number of perspectives. First, relevance is a high-level concept and is therefore difficult to describe numerically using computer bits. Secondly, traditional indexing approaches mostly extract low-level features in a low-level fashion and it therefore difficult to represent relevance using low-level features. Because low-level features bear no correlation to high-level concepts, the burden of relevant retrieval has to be on high-level retrieval strategies, which is again hard. We believe one way in which one can make progress is to develop numerical representations (low-level features) that not only have clear physical meanings but also be related to high-level perceptual concepts. From an engineering point of view, such representation should be easy to compute, efficient to store and which should also render simple and effective retrieval.

In this chapter, the similarity of the images is examined by comparing the variation among the pixels within and between the images, and the spectrum of energy between the query and target images. To test the variations among the pixels within and between the images, the F-ratio test is adopted, and to test the spectrum of energy between the query and target images, the Welch's t-test, i.e. test for equality of two means is employed. If either the query or the target image is treated as a sample, the other is treated as population. By testing the query and target images, it is inferred that whether there is variation and interaction among the pixels within and between the images. If the F-ratio test and the Welch's t-test pass, then it is concluded that the two images are same or similar; otherwise, it is assumed that they differ.

2.2 TESTS FOR SIMILARITY OF IMAGES

Generally, when capturing an image through camera (digital or analog) or scanning through scanner, there are many possibilities to include noise in the image. The inclusion of noise is a random process, which is independent and identically distributed Gaussian random variable. As discussed in Chapter 1, let *X* be a random variable that represents the intensity value with additive noise of a pixel at location (k, l) in a colour image. Hence, an image is assumed to be Gaussian Markov Random field [Kris07, Seet07]. The pixel $X(k, l) \in \Re^3$ is a linear combination of three colours, namely, red, green, and blue, i.e. X (k, l) = {r(k, l), g(k, l), b(k, l). The mean intensity value of each colour is represented by μ, and the variation is denoted by σ^2.

The normal density function of X (k, l) for each colour is given by

$$\frac{1}{\sigma\sqrt{2\Pi}} \exp\left(-(x-\mu)^2\, 2\sigma^2\right), -\infty<x, \mu<\infty, \sigma>0 \qquad \ldots (2.1)$$

The density function in equation (2.1) can be denoted as,

$N(x/\mu, \sigma^2)$ and the distribution law as $N(\mu, \sigma^2)$.

2.2.1 Test Statistic for Interaction among the Pixels within and Between Images

The F-ratio test [Rand12][Ruxt06] is used to test the equality of variations or interactions among the pixels in the query and target images. Let the intensity values F_q =

$(f_q^1, f_q^2, ..., f_q^n)$ and $Ft = (f_t^1, f_t^2, ..., f_t^n)$of the query and target images be independent and identically distributed samples from two normal populations. In order to test the variations or interactions among the pixels within query or target image(s), and variations between the query and target images, the F-ration test is performed. The test statistic is expressed as in Equation (2.2).

The test of the hypothesis is framed for two-tailed test is as follows.

Hypotheses:

H_0: $\sigma_q = \sigma_t$ (Similarity)

H_a: $\sigma_q \neq \sigma_t$ (Non-similarity)

$$F = \frac{\sigma_q^2}{\sigma_t^2} \quad \text{... (2.2)}$$

Let

$$\sigma_q^2 = \frac{1}{n_q - 1} \sum_{i=1}^{n_q} \left(f_q^i - f\right)^2 \text{ and} \quad \text{... (2.3)}$$

$$\sigma_t^2 = \frac{1}{n_t - 1} \sum_{i=1}^{n_t} \left(f_t^i - f\right)^2 \text{ and} \quad \text{... (2.4)}$$

be the sample variances of the query and target images respectively. Let

$$\overline{f_q} = \frac{1}{n_q} \sum_{i=1}^{\Pi_q} f_q^i \quad \text{... (2.6)}$$

and

$$\overline{f_t} = \frac{1}{n_t} \sum_{i=1}^{n_t} / \text{it} \quad \text{... (2.6)}$$

be the sample means of the query and target images respectively; n_q and n_t are the number of pixels in the query and target images respectively; f_q and f_t are the standard deviations of the query and target images.

Critical Region: If the F-ratio value is less than the critical value, $F\alpha$, n_q-1, n_t-1, with degrees of freedom n_q-1 and n_t-1, and the significance level α, it is inferred that the query and target images are same or similar; otherwise, it is concluded that the two images differ. The critical value F_α is referred to the F distribution in the statistical table.

2.2.2 Test for Equality of Spectrum of Energy between the Query and Target Images

As discussed in the previous section, if the interaction among the pixels' intensity values between the query and target images passes the test, then it is proceeded to test the equality of spectrum of energy between the query and target images with the basic assumption that there is no variation among the intensity values between the query and target images. After observing the outcome of the two tests, it is concluded that the two images are same or not. To achieve this, the test for equality of means, i.e. Welch's t-test is performed on the images. The tests of hypotheses are assumed to be as follows:

If the test for equality of variances and the means manifest that the query and target images pass the tests, such as F-ratio and Welch's t-test, it is concluded that the two images are same or similar; otherwise, it is assumed that they belongs to different groups. The Welch's test statistics is expressed as in equation (2.7), which compares the mean values of the query and target images. The test of the hypothesis is framed for two-tailed test is as follows.

H_0: $\mu_q = \mu_t$ (Similarity)

H_a: $\mu_q \neq \mu_t$ (Non-similarity)

$$Wt = \frac{\mu_q - \mu_t}{\sqrt{\frac{s_q^2}{n_q} + \frac{s_t^2}{n_t}}} \qquad \text{... (2.7)}$$

The μ_q and μ_t are mean values of the query and target images that can be computed using the expression presented in equations (2.5) and (2.6) respectively. The s_q^2 and s_t^2 are the sample variances of the query and target images respectively those can be computed using the expressions in equations (2.3) and (2.4). The variances of the query and target images are computed individually separately. The degrees of freedom, v, is calculated using the formula given in equation (2.8), which is used to refer to the statistical table for the significant level α.

$$v = \frac{\left(\frac{s_q^2}{n_q} + \frac{s_t^2}{n_t}\right)^2}{\left(\frac{\frac{s_q^2}{n_q}}{n_q - 1}\right)^2 + \left(\frac{\frac{s_t^2}{n_t}}{n_t - 1}\right)^2} \qquad \text{... (2.8)}$$

***Critical Region*:** If the WT value is less than the critical value, $t_{(\alpha, v)}$, with degrees of freedom, v, and the significance level α, it is inferred that the query and target images belongs to the same class. Otherwise, it is concluded that they belongs to different classes of image datasets. The critical value tα is referred to as the t-distribution in the statistical table. The implementation of these two statistical tests are discussed as detailed in Chapter 5.

CHAPTER 3

MULTIVARIATE PARAMETRIC STATISTICAL TESTS OF HYPOTHESES FOR SIMILARITY OF IMAGES

3.1 INTRODUCTION

In this Chapter, the distance measure, Chernoff distance is adopted for matching and retrieving the images from image repositories. The distance measures play a significant role in matching and retrieving images, especially in the CBIR systems.

The distance measures can be categorized into pairwise (point-wise comparison) approach and distribution approach (massive comparison). The former is precise and simple, but it is not robust for rotation and scaling, while the latter is robust, and at the same time it is effective and efficient. Moreover, in the case of latter, a user can match and retrieve a number of images as his/her choice by fixing significance level of the test statistic. This is not possible in the case of former, since there is no such an option; thus, the user has to select same or similar images from the list of retrieved images.

A number of works have been developed based on the statistical distributional approach and tests of hypothesis; most of them are Gaussian distribution-based approach. In general, an image should have distributed to either Gaussian process or non-Gaussian process or even distribution free; so we simply cannot apply the parametric tests. Because the parametric tests can be employed only if an image is distributed to Gaussian process; otherwise the non-parametric test statistic is appropriate. Thus, we have to examine whether an image is distributed to Gaussian process or not. This is the additional computational head-ache to the retrieval process. To avoid this, the Chernoff distance measure is employed, since it adapts itself, despite the images are distributed to Gaussian process or non-Gaussian or even if it is distribution free.

Many researchers have used Bhattacharyya distance (BD) [Kail67, Ray89, Choi03] and Kullback-Liebler distance (KLD) measures in control theory and signal processing for feature extraction and comparing the distance between two distributions.

The work proposed in [Ali66, Csis67] reports that the divergence 'div', between any two probability distributions, P_1 and P_2, should satisfy the following properties: $div(P_1, P_2) \geq 0$, and $div(P_1 , P_2) = 0$ if and only if $P_1 = P_2$. The latter reveals that the Two probability distributions are equal if there is no divergence (distance) between them and vice versa. In the case of Bhattacharyya distance, the probabilities of two distributions are assumed to be equal, i.e. $P_1 = P_2 = 1/2$ [Fuku90]. This means that both distributions have equal probabilities, with optimum value 1/2. But, in the case of real-life images, there is no such assurance.

Thus, in the context of image retrieval, the Bhattacharyya distance metric will yield moderate results than other existing metrics.

As suggested in [Choi03], the BD measure is superior to the KLD measure in terms of time complexity. But there are some difficulties in using the BD measures, i.e. the BD measure can be employed to extract features, and compare two images only if they are distributed to Gaussian process; otherwise, it cannot be applied. Zhang, et al. [Zhan11] suggest that there are some obstacles on assuming the images as a Gaussian process. Abou - Moustafa, et al. [Mous12] report that the BD and KLD measures do not satisfy all metric axioms necessary for many algorithms. Thus, they propose a modification on the KLD and the BD; then it transforms the two measures into distance metrics. Even after the modification, they do not yield better results. The Chernoff distance (CD) measure overcomes this difficulties, since it adjusts itself and performs well. The BD is a special case of the CD measure, and also the CD measure becomes Mahalanobis distance (MD) while the covariance matrices of the two images are same (for more details the readers can refer to APPENDIX). The BD [Fuku90] and KLD are not metrics [Cove91], since they violate at least one of the distance axioms. Johnson and Johnson and Sinanovic [John01] analyse the distance measures - KLD, CD, and BD - and suggest that the CD is better than the BD. Hence, it is believed that the CD measure will lead to better results than the KLD, BD, and MD measures. Kokare, et al. [Koka03] perform a comparison of nine similarity measures such as Manhattan, Weighted-Mean-Variance, Euclidean, Chebychev, Mahalanobis, Canberra, Bray-Curtis, Squared-Chord, and Squared Chi-square distances, and report that the Canberra and Bray-Curtis distance measures give better results than the Euclidean and Mahalanobis distance measures. But, they consider only texture images for the experiment, and do not discuss about the rotation, scaling, and noise. In [Koka03], most of the distance measures discussed are based on point processing except Mahalanobis and Weighted-Mean-Variance distances. In the case of MD, if we put $M_q = M_t = M$ in Equation (A.3), then the MD becomes zero. It means that there is no distance between the two distributions, i.e. the two distributions are same. Since the Mahalanobis distance metric fully depends on the mean value of the distributions, the decision taken based on the distance can lead to wrong results.

Generally, though the mean vectors of the two distributions are equal, there is no constraint that the covariance matrices are to be same. In such case, it is not possible for the two distributions to be same. This is the main drawback of the MD measure. Thus, it gives a poor result when compared to others methods as reported in [Koka03].

Motivation: It is observed from the literature that most of the works assume either a whole image or the segmented regions of an image are assumed to be Gaussian random field. But, this is not applicable for all types of images, because even the texture images may be distributed to non-Gaussian process. This is depicted in Figure 3.1. As we discussed earlier, in this context, the parametric statistical tests do not yield better results. In this study, an attempt is made to test whether the texture images are distributed to either Gaussian process or mixed or other than the Gaussian process or distribution free. In order to examine this, a manifold texture images are included in the test. The outcome of the test reveals that most of the texture images, either natural or artificial, are not distributed as independent and identical to Gaussian process. For a sample, due to space constraint, only two of the images considered for the experiment and the histogram obtained for them are presented in Figure 3.1.The results reveal that the images presented in Figure 3.1 are not distributed to Gaussian process, because they do not follow the symmetric property of the Gaussian distribution, i.e. the image presented in Figure 3.1(a) is skewed to left tail, and the image presented in Figure 3.1(b) is skewed to right tail. In such a case, the BD measure is not appropriate; so it does not give better results. In this context the CD measure can be adopted, since it adapts itself to the nature of the images (either the image is distributed to Gaussian or mixed or other than the Gaussian or even if it is distribution free), and so it yields better results than the BD measure. In this research work, it is believed that in some cases a segmented region of the image does not follow the Gaussian process because entire or almost all the pixel intensity values are same. For instance, let us consider the cheek region of the lady's head image presented in Figure 5.6 of the Chapter 5. The pixel intensity values in the cheek might be distributed to uniform process (uniformly distributed - follows uniform distribution), since almost all the pixel intensity values are same in the region. This motivated us to develop the proposed research work. The obtained results are presented in Chapter 5, and the results show that the CD measure outperforms the OP method, KLD, BD, and MD measures.

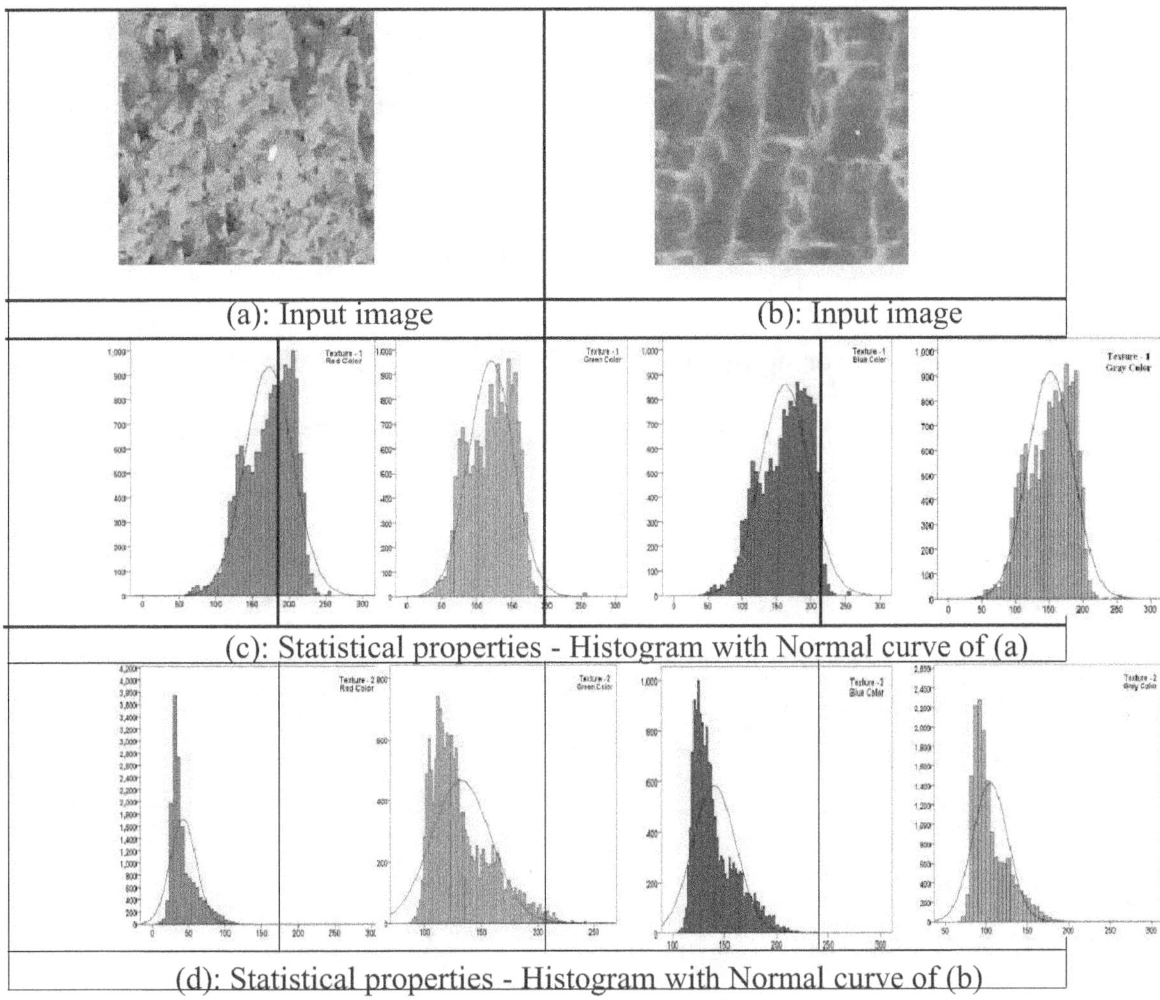

Figure 3.1: Texture images and their distributional properties

Overview of the Proposed Method

First, the proposed method performs a pre-process on the input query image, viz. removes outliers or noise. The pre-processing is discussed in detailed in the next Chapter. The query image is examined to know whether it is texture or structure. If the query image is a structure, then it is segmented into various regions according to its nature, and the regions are counted; if the number of regions in the query and target images match, then it is proceeded to the Chernoff test; otherwise, it is inferred that the two images are different. If the query image is texture, it is considered as it is. The CD measure discussed in section 2.2.1 is applied on the noise removed images. The CD between the query and target images is tested at a desired significance level, and if the distance is minimal then it is inferred that the two images are same or similar.

The same or similar images are marked and indexed in ascending order.

The overall procedure of the proposed method is illustrated in Figure 3.2.

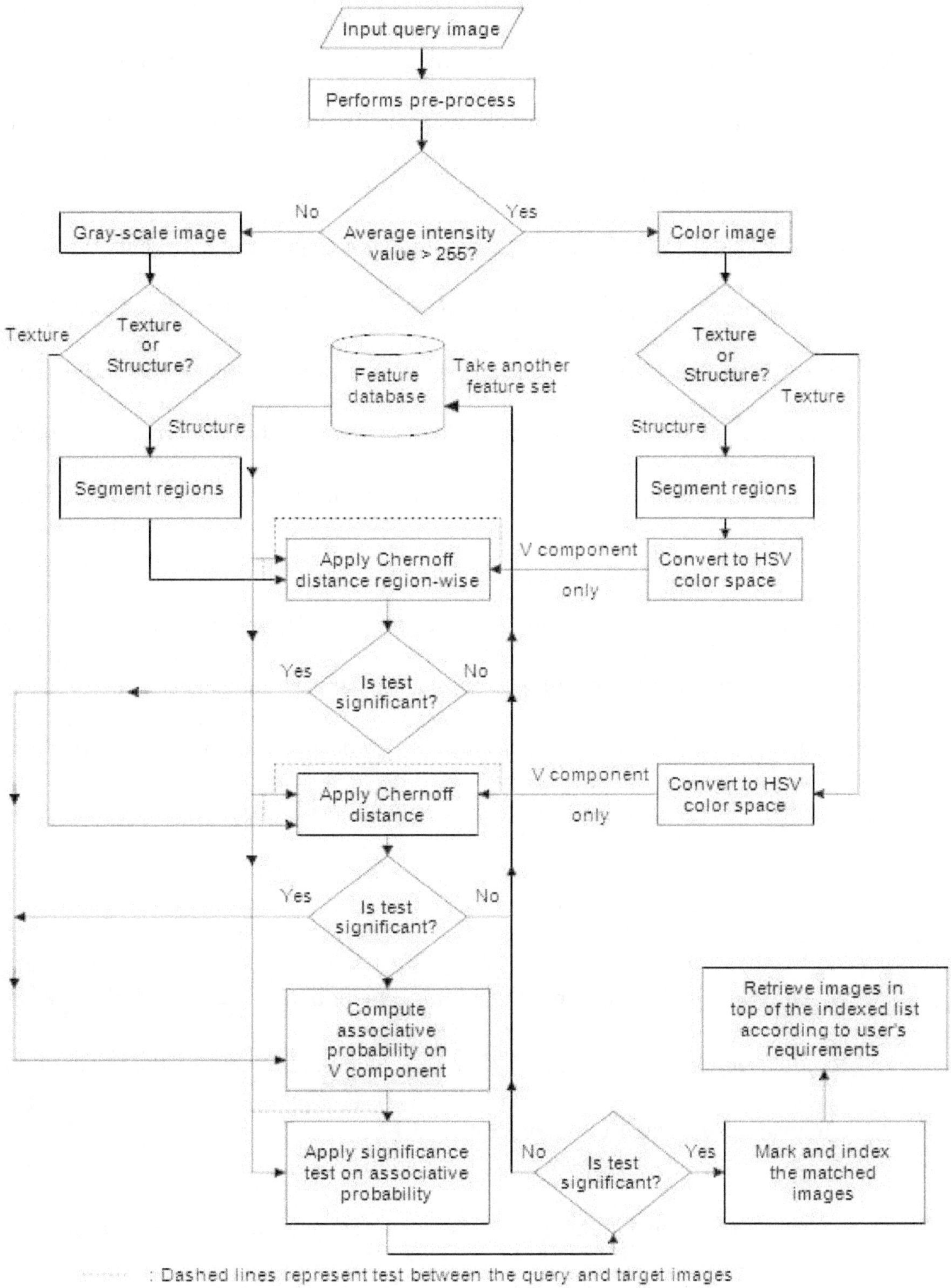

Figure 3.2: Overview of the Proposed Work

3.2 PROPOSED IMAGE RETRIEVAL METHODS

In the case of real-life images and automated image retrieval system, it is difficult to understand that the image follows which distribution, but it might follow a certain distribution function. It may be a Gaussian or a mixture of two distributions or even it may be a distribution free, but need not be distributed to a Gaussian function. In such cases, the BD, KLD, and MD measures are not appropriate, because these measures adhere to Gaussian properties. But in such a case, the CD measure could be applied because it adapts itself even though the normality is not in place [Duda00]. This is also one of the reasons why the proposed method is a fully automated one. Let *f* be a random process function that represents the intensity value with additive noise of a pixel at location (k, l) in a color image. The pixel $f(k, l) \in \Re^3$ is a linear combination of three colors, such as red, green, and blue, i.e. $f(k, l) = [r(k, l), g(k, l), b(k, l)]^T$, where T represents the transformation of the vector. The mean intensity value of each color is represented in vector forms by the notations M_r, M_g and M_b; and the covariance matrix is denoted by Σ. The multivariate Gaussian density function of $X(k, l)$ is given by

$$\frac{1}{\left(\sqrt{2\Pi}\right)}3\,|\Sigma|\left(\frac{1}{-2}(x-\mu)^T\Sigma^{-1}(x-\mu\right) \qquad \text{... (3.1)}$$

The density function mentioned in Equation (3.1) can be denoted as $n(x/\mu, \Sigma)$, and the distribution law as $N(\mu, \Sigma)$. The i-th diagonal element of the covariance matrix, σ_{ii}, is the variance of the i-th component of $X(k, l)$

The i-th diagonal element σ_{ii} of the covariance matrix Σ is the variance of the i-th component of $f(k, l)$. The mean vector of each color of the pixels in the image is

$$M = E(F) = E \mid M \begin{bmatrix} M_r \\ M_b^g \end{bmatrix} = \begin{bmatrix} m_r \\ m_g \\ m_b \end{bmatrix} \qquad \text{... (3.2)}$$

and the covariance matrix is

$$\Sigma = \begin{bmatrix} \sigma_{rr} & \sigma_{rg}\rho & \sigma_{rb}\rho \\ \sigma_{gr}\rho & \sigma_{gg} & \sigma_{gb}\rho \\ \sigma_{br}\rho & \sigma_{bg}\rho & \sigma_{bb}\rho \end{bmatrix} = \begin{bmatrix} \sigma_r^2 & \sigma_{rg}\rho & \sigma_{rb}\rho \\ \sigma_{gr}\rho & \sigma_g^2 & \sigma_{gb}\rho \\ \sigma_{br}\rho & \sigma_{bg}\rho & \sigma_b^2 \end{bmatrix} \qquad \text{... (3.3)}$$

where, σ_r^2, σ_g^2, and σ_b^2 are the variations among the intensity values of red, green, and blue colors respectively; σ_{rg} represents the interaction between the red and green colors; likewise, σ_{rb} and σ_{gb} represent the interaction between the corresponding colors; ρ represents the correlation or the interrelationship between the corresponding color pixels. The covariance matrix, $\mathbf{\Sigma}$, is symmetric and positive definite.

3.2.1 Proposed Distance Measure for Similarity of Images

Let us assume $f_{(c)}^{(q)}(k, l)$ and $f_{(c)}^{(t)}(k, l)$ be the intensity values of the c-th color (c = 1, 2, 3: red, green, blue) of a pixel at location (k, l) of the query and target images $F^q(k, l)$ and $F^t(k, l)$ are distributed as independent and identical to Gaussian process with mean vector M and covariance matrix Σ, i.e. $F^q(k, l) \sim N(M_q, \Sigma_q)$ and $F^t(k,l) \sim N(M_t, \Sigma_t)$ with *a priori* probabilities p_q and p_t. The error probability of the upper bound of the Bayes error in a closed-form is defined as in Equation (3.4). The Chernoff distance between the two distributions, $F^q(k, l)$ and $F^t(k, l)$, of the query and target images is defined in Equation (3.5).

$$\int p_q(F^q) p_t(F^t) dF = e^{-CD(P_q, P_t)} \qquad \text{... (3.4)}$$

where,

$$CD\,(Pq, Pt) = \frac{P_q P_t}{2} (M_q - M_t)^T \Sigma_{q,t}^{-1} (M_q - M_t) +$$

$$\frac{1}{2}\left(\log\left|\Sigma_{q,t} - \log\left(\left|\Sigma_q\right| P_q - \log \Sigma_t \left| P_t\right.\right)\right.\right) \qquad \text{... (3.5)}$$

$$\text{where, } P_q = \frac{N_q}{N_q + N_t} \text{ and } P_t = \frac{N_t}{N_q + N_t}; 0 \le P_q, P_t \le 1; \qquad \text{... (3.6)}$$

$$\Sigma_{q,t} = P_q \Sigma_q + P_t \Sigma_t; \qquad \text{... (3.7)}$$

$$\Sigma \sqrt{P_q P_t} = 1 \text{ and} \qquad \text{... (3.8)}$$

$$\frac{dCD(P_q, P_t)}{d(P_q, P_t)} = \frac{1 - 2P_q}{2} (M_q - M_t)T\ \Sigma_{q,t}^{-1} (M_q - M_t) = 0 \qquad \text{... (3.9)}$$

P_q and P_t are *a priori* probabilities of the query and target images, and P_q, $P_t \in [0, 1]$; M_q and M_t are the mean vectors of the query and target images; M_q and M_t are covariance matrices; F^q (k, l) and F^t (k, l) are the functions of the query and target images; P_q^i and P_t^i represent the probability values of the pixels in the query and target images respectively, where i=1, 2, $N_{(.)}$.

Significance and Matching

If $CD(P_q, P_t) \le 1 - \alpha$, at the level of significance $\alpha = \Sigma\sqrt{P_q P_t}$, then it is inferred that the query and target images are same or similar; otherwise, the two images differ. Based on the outcome of the inference, the matched images, such as same or similar, are marked and indexed in ascending order, and the indexed images are retrieved. The significance level, α, is fixed after conducting a rigorous experiment with various types of images, such as texture (both stochastic and periodic) and untexture or structure.

The proposed method, based on the CD measure, has three main advantages:

i. It adapts itself to all types of images, i.e. the images follow either Gaussian or mixed or non-Gaussian process because *a priori* probabilities, P_q and P_t, of the query and target images play a noteworthy role in measuring the distance between them; The P_q and P_t are computed, based on the query and target images, they are not fixed to 1/2 as in BD.

ii. In the case of BD, the *a priori* probabilities, P_q and P_t, of the query and target images are fixed to 1/2, which is optimal [Fuku90, Rued08]; so they must adhere to the Gaussian properties. In the case of image retrieval, the *a priori* probability of the query image which matches with the target image is fixed to 1/2. It is biased because the image may or may not adhere to the Gaussian properties In the case of fully automated image retrieval system, it is difficult to understand the nature or structure of an image without analysis; and it is not fair to fix the *a priori* probability of P_q to 1/2. Thus, the BD is not appropriate for all types of images; so it does not lead to a better result. In the case of CD, the *a priori* probability of P_q is estimated by solving the expression in Equation (3.9) according to the nature of the query image. So the proposed method works well for any type of images, even though they are distributed to either Gaussian or mixed or non-Gaussian random process or even if it is distribution free. Thus, the proposed method leads to better results than those of the existing methods. A detailed discussion of the implementation of the theory concepts is presented in

Chapter 5.

3.3 POSITION VECTORS AND ORTHOGONALITY

Furthermore, to validate the effectiveness and efficiency of the proposed method, position vectors are computed, and the *cosine*-direction-based orthogonality test is performed on the position vectors. The position vectors are computed using the associative probability of the pixel values. Let the query and target images are assumed to be two distribution functions, f_q and f_t. The associated probabilities, P_1^q, P_2^q, P_n^q and P_1^t, P_2^t, P_n^t, of the query and target images are computed. The sum of probabilities of each distribution is 1, i.e. $\Sigma_n^1 P_t^{iq}$ and $\Sigma_1^n P_i^t=1$. The position vectors, $\left(\sqrt{P_1^q}\ \sqrt{P_2^q}\ \sqrt{P_n^q}\right)$ and $\left(\sqrt{P_1^t}\ \sqrt{P_2^t}\ \sqrt{P_n^t}\right)$, of the query and target images are computed, and used to measure the angle between the two images. The position vectors are also used to measure the *cosine* direction of the vectors in *n*-dimensional space referred to as a system of orthogonal coordinate axes. Based on these vectors, the divergence (angle between images) of the two images is computed using the expression given in Equation (5.10).

$$\cos\theta = \left(\frac{\sqrt{P_i^q}}{\left\|\sqrt{P_i^q}\right\|}\right)\left(\frac{\sqrt{P_i^t}}{\left\|\sqrt{P_i^t}\right\|}\right) \qquad \text{... (3.10)}$$

The expressions in numerator and denominator represent *dot-product* and *product of modulus* of two vectors respectively. If $\cos(\theta) = 0$, it means that the vectors are orthogonal (i.e. $\theta = 90^o$), i.e. the query and target images are absolutely different, whereas the two images are co-linear, i.e. same, if $\cos(\theta)=1$ (i.e. $\theta = 0^o$). The implementation of the theory concepts is illustrated in Chapter 5.

3.4 DATASET USED

Caltech 256 : Caltech is another image data set, created in 2007. It is a successor to Caltech 101. It is intended to address some of the weaknesses of Caltech 101. Overall, it is a more difficult data set than Caltech 101, but it suffers from comparable problems. It includes

- 30,607 images, covering a larger number of categories
- Minimum number of images per category raised to 80
- Images are not left-right aligned
- More variation in image presentation

VisTex Dataset : The Vision Texture (VisTex) dataset is prepared by the Massachusetts Institute of Technology (MIT) [12]. The dataset is not only consisting of homogeneous frontal acquisition of textures, it also comes with real-world scenes with multiple textures and video textures. The database was created with the intention of providing a large set of high quality textures for computer vision applications.

INRAI Dataset: • Descriptors with size equal to (526MB). • Images: jpg1.tar.gz and jpg2.tar.gz (1.1GB and 1.6 GB). • Visual dictionaries (100, 200, 500, 1K, 2K, 5K, 10K, 20K, 50K, 100K and 200K visual words, 144MB) learned on Flickr60K. • Descriptors of Flickr60K (independent dataset, 636MB). • Pre-computed features for one million images, stored in 1000 archives of 1000 feature files each (235GB in total occupied).

APPENDIX

$$CD(P_{qt}, P) = \frac{P_q\, P_t}{2}\,(M_q - M_t)^T\, \Sigma_{q,t}^{-1}\,(M_q - M_t) + \frac{1}{2}\left(\log\left|\Sigma_{q,t}\right| - \log\left|\Sigma_q\right|P_q - \log\left|\Sigma_t\right|P_t\right) \quad \text{... (A.1)}$$

CHAPTER 4

EXPERIMENTAL SETUP

4.1 INTRODUCTION

Nevertheless, nowadays, a number of image databases are available, in this research work, we have designed and constructed our own image database with the help of different types of images; and we have constructed its feature database to examine the proposed retrieval system. The main aim of constructing our own and independent image database is to form a database with a heterogeneous group of images such as texture, untexture or structure, multi-spectral or hyper-spectral images, and these images may also be both in colour or gray-scale. Since the newly constructed image database contains manifold images, empirical study of the proposed techniques emphasis the efficiency and effectiveness of the proposed system. The images incorporated into the image database have been pre-processed. A pre-processing method is incorporated into the proposed research work, which is discussed in detaile in section 4.4 of this Chapter. The following sections discuss the designs of image database and its feature database construction.

4.2 GENERAL IMAGE DATABASE

In order to experiment the proposed method, an image database is constructed using 127167 images, which have been collected from different sources, and are subjected to experiments. Among them, 1829 color images of size 512×512 pixels have been collected from various sources such as 4656 images from CalTech image database [Sala11]; 673 images from Corel image database; 3296 images from INRIA Holidays image database [Duda00]; 659 images from VisTex image database; 508 images with size 128×128 that are photographed by a digital camera; 517 images with size 128×128 that have been downloaded from various websites. The texture images collected from Corel and VisTex image databases are divided into 16 non-overlapping sub-images of size 128×128. To validate that the proposed method is robust for rotation, scaling and noise, the images are rotated through 90°, 180° and 270° degrees, and scaled. Furthermore, to emphasize the efficiency of the proposed system, a number of different types of noisy images are considered in the experiment. For a sample, the noisy images are presented in Figure 3. In addition to that 524 multi- spectral satellite images such as Tropical depression and Cyclone images, and wetland images are incorporated in the image database. Therefore, totally there are [1829 (actual image) + ((16 × (673+659)) + (4656 + 3296 + 508 + 517)) × 3 (rotated through 90°, 180° and 270°) +30,289 (scaled) + 524 (satellite)] = 127167 images. Based on these image collections, an image database and feature vector (FV) database are constructed. The texture images collected from Brodatz, Corel, and VisTex image databases are divided into 16 non-overlapping sub-images of size 128×128. For a sample, an image and its grid has been presented in Figure 4.1. To examine the proposed system is invariant for rotation, scaling, and noise, the images are rotated through 90°, 180° and 270° degrees and scaled, and also a few number of noised images are included. Based on these image collections, an image database and its feature database are constructed.

(a)

(b)

Figure 4.1: (a): whole image; (b): grid images

4.3 FEATURE DATABASE CONSTRUCTION AND INDEXING

The coefficient of variation (CV) is computed on the input query image using the expression given in Equation (4.1), and the CV is compared to a threshold value t. If CV > t, then it is assumed that the query image is structure, and if CV < t, then the query image is assumed to be texture. The threshold t is fixed at 20 percent, i.e. the CV value is 0.20. The threshold ***t*** is fixed after conducting a rigorous empirical analysis. For a sample, a few of them with CV are presented in Figure 4.2. If the query image is structure, then it is segmented into various regions according to its shape and structure; otherwise, it is treated as a texture image, and the whole (not segmented) image is subjected to experiments. If the query image is color, then it is modelled to HSV color space; otherwise, the image is assumed to be gray-scale, and considered for the experiment as it is. The proposed method is employed on H, S, and V components individually for extracting image features as discussed in Chapter 3. On each region, sample size N_t, mean vector M_t, and covariance matrix Σ_t of the target images are computed, and they are combined together including the number of objects π_t in the image; and they are formed as a FV database. The extracted features are classified into various groups according to their nature using fuzzy *c-means* algorithm [Lin14]. For each group, median value is calculated; based on the median, the FVs are indexed. Based on the classes of the FVs, images in the database are classified into different groups, and it establishes a link between the images and their corresponding FVs of each class. Now, the extracted FVs of the query image are compared to those of the index of the FVs in the image feature database, and the same or similar images are identified using the methods discussed in Chapters 2 and 3. Then the identified image and its FVs are grouped into the corresponding class. If the FVs of the query image do not match with any classes of the FV database, then it is formed into a new FV class.

$$\text{Coefficient of Variation (CV)} = \frac{\sigma}{f} \qquad \dots (4.1)$$

Structure Images						
CV	0.3949	0.5924	0.2636	0.2931	0.5084	0.5345
Texture Images	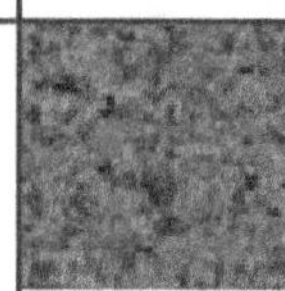	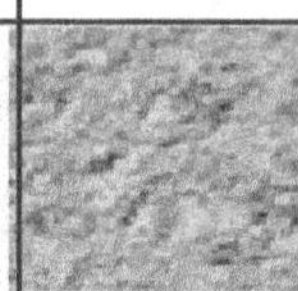	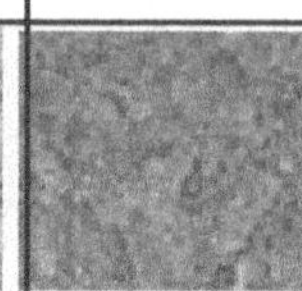	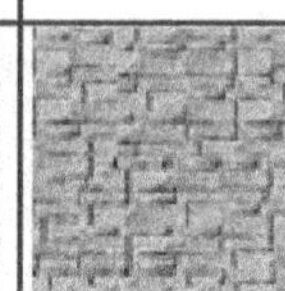	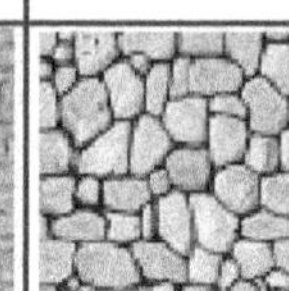	
CV	0.2251	0.1923	0.1539	0.2063	0.2038	0.1291

Figure 4.2: Coefficient of Variation for Structure and Texture images

4.4 PRE-PROCESSING

The presence of noise in the image data may lead to less precision of retrieval. Thus, it is indispensable to remove the noise before performing the feature extraction process. In order to remove the noise, the proposed method adopts a pre-processing technique, which is proposed in [Liu14], which improves the efficacy of the proposed retrieval method even if the images are rigorously affected by various types of noise. A brief description of the noise removal method proposed in [Liu14] is presented here.

$$\| f^2 - q \| \leq r^2, \qquad \dots (4.2)$$

$$r^2 = | f_u - q |^2 = K(f_u, fu) + K(q, q) - 2K(f_u, q) \qquad \dots (4.3)$$

$$r^2 = K(f_u, f_u) + \sum_{i=1}^{p+n} \sum_{k=1}^{p+1} \beta_i \beta_k K(f_j, f_k) - \sum_{i=1}^{p+n} 2 \Sigma\beta_i (f_i, fu) \qquad \dots (4.4)$$

where, $q = \sum_{i=1}^{p+n} \beta i \, \theta(f_i)$, β is Lagrange multiplier; $\theta(f_i)$ is a vector of the pixel intensity values; f is pixel intensity value to be classified whether it is affected by noise or not. To classify a pixel intensity value f, its distance to the centroid of the hyper-sphere is calculated. If this distance is less than or equal to r, i.e. satisfies the condition in equation (4.2), then f is accepted as the normal data; otherwise, it is identified as a noise. After performing the pre-processing method, by which the noises in the images are removed, the images are incorporated into the image database.

4.5 PERFORMANCE MEASURE

In order to measure the performance of the proposed method, the F_β-measure is adopted, which is a harmonic mean of precision (P) and recall (R) values, and that are given in Equations (5.1), (5.2) and (5.3). The F_β measures the effectiveness of retrieval with respect to a user who attaches β times as much importance to recall as precision [Powe11]. The β value is decided with respect to weight given to the P and R. In the context of the proposed research work, the β is considered as 0.5, since more weight is given to the precision. Thus, Equation (5.1) is rewritten as in Equation (5.4).

$$F_\beta \text{ measure} = (1+\beta^2) \times \frac{(P).(R)}{(\beta^2 \times P)+(R)} \quad \text{... (4.5)}$$

where,

$$P = \frac{|\{\text{Re levant Im ages}\}\{\text{Re trieved Im ages}\}|}{|\text{Re trieved Im ages}|} \quad \text{... (4.6)}$$

$$R = \frac{|\{\text{Re levant Im ages}\}\{\text{Re trieved Im ages}\}|}{|\text{Re trieved Im ages}|} \quad \text{... (4.7)}$$

$$F \text{ measure} = (1+0.5^2) \times \frac{(R)\times(R)}{(0.5^2 \times P)+(R)} \quad \text{... (4.8)}$$

CHAPTER 5

EXPERIMENTS AND RESULTS

5.1 INTRODUCTION

In order to experiment and validate the proposed statistical methods, F-ratio test and Welch's t-test discussed in Chapter 2, and the Chernoff distance measure discussed in Chapter 3; the image and feature databases designed and constructed in Chapter 4 are considered. To improve and strengthen the retrieval performance of the proposed method, the images included in the database are subjected to pre-process. To evaluate and emphasis the efficacy and effectiveness of the proposed method, the F-measure is used. The F-measure is calculated based on precision and recall values.

5.2 IMAGE MATCHING, INDEXING AND RETRIEVAL

The structure images, normally, are not distributed to Gaussian process, and it can be mixture of Gaussian process or other than Gaussian process. For a sample and illustration, the normal curve is drawn, and is presented in Figure 5.8 for the texture images; and normal curve is drawn for the structured image, tiger images presented Figure 1.3, that are presented in Figures 1.4 and 1.5. Thus, the input query images checked whether it is structured or not. If it is structured, then the structures or shapes in the image are segmented into various regions as discussed in Chapter 4. If the query image is textured, then it is considered for the experiment as it is. The shapes in the structured images are segmented by simply subtracting the colour information from each other. For instance, the information of red colour content can be segmented by subtracting the information of green and blue colours content from gray colour content. For an example, the segmented shapes of the tiger and house images are presented in

Figures 5.1 and 5.2.

(a): actual image | (b): segmented shapes

Figure 5.1: Segmented shapes of tiger image

(d) (e) (f)

Figure 5.2: Segmented sha pes: (a): actual image; (b): red component; (c): green component; (d): blue component; (e): combination of green and blue; (f): combination of red and green

5.2.1 Bivariate Statistical Methods

Firstly, the input query image is subjected for a pre-processing, viz. noise removal. To remove noises, the method discussed in section 4.4 of the Chapter 4 is employed, and the results obtained are presented in Figure 5.9.

In this section, a novel method based on bivariate statistical methods: F-ratio test and Welch's t-test, which are discussed in Chapter 3 implemented here for retrieving the target images. The F-ratio test statistic is used to test the equality of variances of the query and target images while the spectrum of energy between the same images are examined by the Welch's t-test. If the query and target images pass the test for equality of variances and test for spectrum energy, in this study it is concluded that the two images are same or similar. In the proposed technique, mean and variance (first and second order moments of the sample points) are used as representatives of both query and target images. The methods proposed in [Kris12, Han07] retrieve only the texture images with intensity values ranging from 0-255, i.e. gray-scale images. This motivated us to develop a new method which retrieves colour images; both texture and structure images; and invariant for rotation and scaling. In this research work, we have made an attempt to use F-ratio test and Welch's t-test statistics in straight to retrieve the images.

An empirical study is conducted on the image database designed and constructed, based on the statistical tests of hypotheses discussed in Chapters 2 and 3, those examine the performance of the proposed test statistics. As discussed earlier, the input query image is segmented into various regions according to its nature and shapes as presented in Figures 5.1 and 5.2 in section 5.2, if it is structured. Otherwise, it is treated as textured image, and the whole image is considered as it is for the experiments. The segmented image is modelled to HSV colour model, and the V component is considered for the statistical tests of hypothesis. The number of regions of the query and target images matches, the experiment is proceeded to perform the F-ratio and Welch's tests. First, the query and target images are included in the test for the equality of variances, viz. F-ratio test, and they pass the test; then it is proceeded to the test the equality of spectrum of energy, i.e. Welch's test, the same images also pass the test, then it is concluded that the two images are same or similar. Otherwise, the images are different.

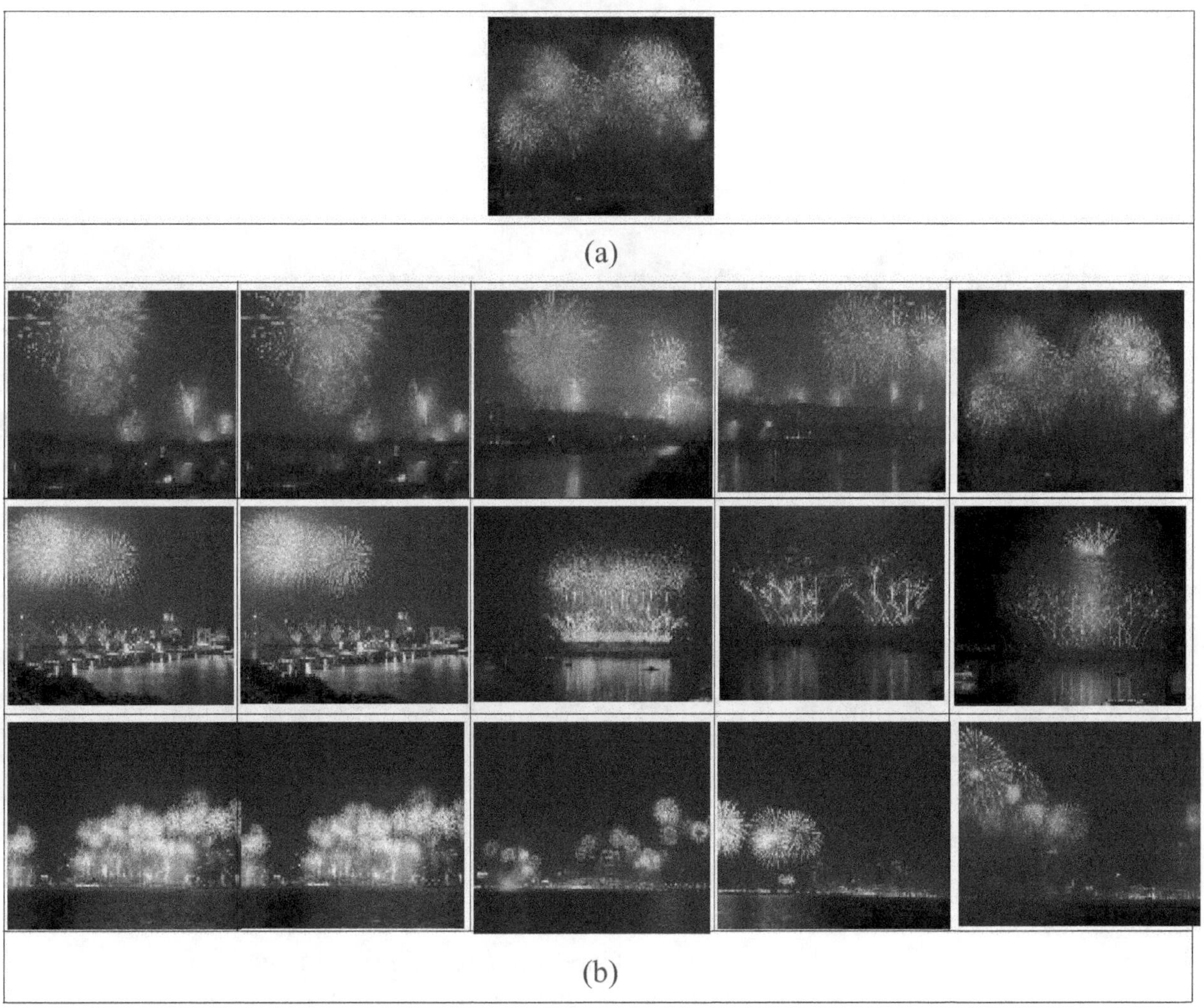

Figure 5.3: Corel images - texture or semi-structured images.
(a): input query image; (b): columns 1-5: retrieved images

The image in Figure 5.3(a) is submitted as input to the system, and the experiment is conducted at various significance levels. The system returns the images in row 1 of the Figure 5.3(b), while the level of significance is fixed at 10 percent; while the significance level is at 15 percent, the system retrieves the images in row 3 of the Figure 5.3(b); and at the level of significance 20 percent, the system retrieves the images in row 2 of the Figure 5.3(b).

(a)

(b)

Figure 5.4: Corel images: building images.
(a): input query images; (b): retrieved output images

Furthermore, to prove that the system works well for the structured images, the Oxford building image presented in Figure 5.4(a) is considered as input. The system retrieves the images in columns 1 to 3 of the Figure 5.4(b) at the level of significance 12 percent; the system returns the images in column 4 of the Figure 5.4(b), while the significance level is fixed at 20 percent.

The Holiday's images are considered for the experiment, the images presented in column 1 of the Figure 5.5 are inputted to the system; the system responses with the images in columns 2 to 5, while the significance level is fixed at 15 percent. The images in column 2 are retrieved at the level of significance 1 percent; the system returns the images in column 3 and 4, while the level of significance is fixed at 12 percent; and the images are returned when the significance level is at 15 percent.

Figure 5.5: Holiday's images.
Column 1: input query images; Columns 2 - 5: retrieved target images

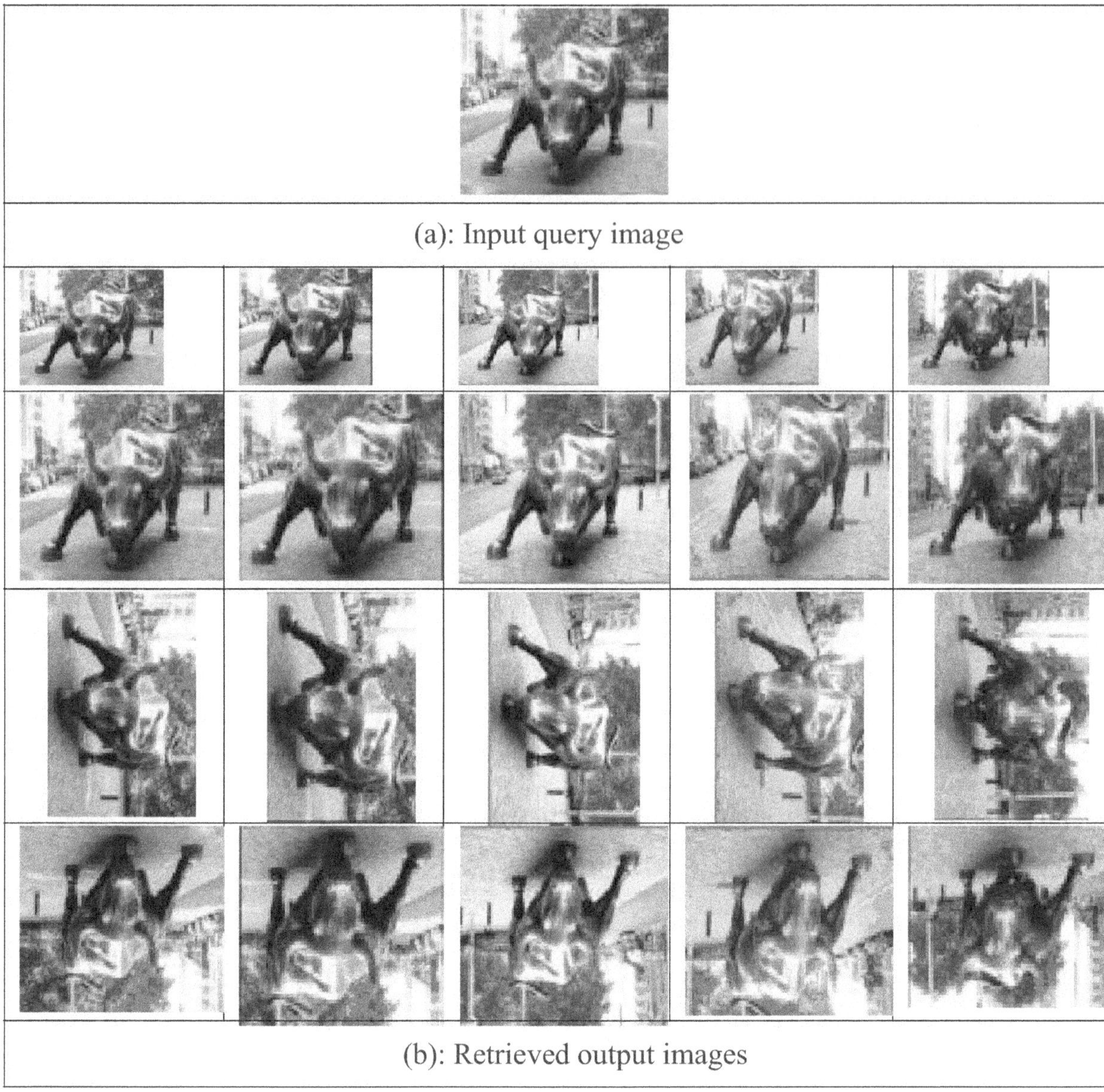

Figure 5.6: Wall Street Bull - downloaded from internet. (a): Input query image; (b): Retrieved output images: row 1 - scaled down image of size 75 × 100; row 2 actual image with size 96 × 128; row 3 - images in row 2 are rotated clockwise by 90 degrees; row 4 - images in row 2 are rotated clockwise by 180 degrees

Furthermore to emphasis the proposed method is robust for rotation and scaling, the image in Figure 5.6(a) is inputted, and the system responses with the images in Figure 5.6(b). The images in column 1 are returned, while the level of significance is fixed at 1 percent; at the level of significance 5 percent, the images in columns 2 and 3 are retrieved; while the significance level is at 12 percent, the system returns the images in columns 4 and 5.

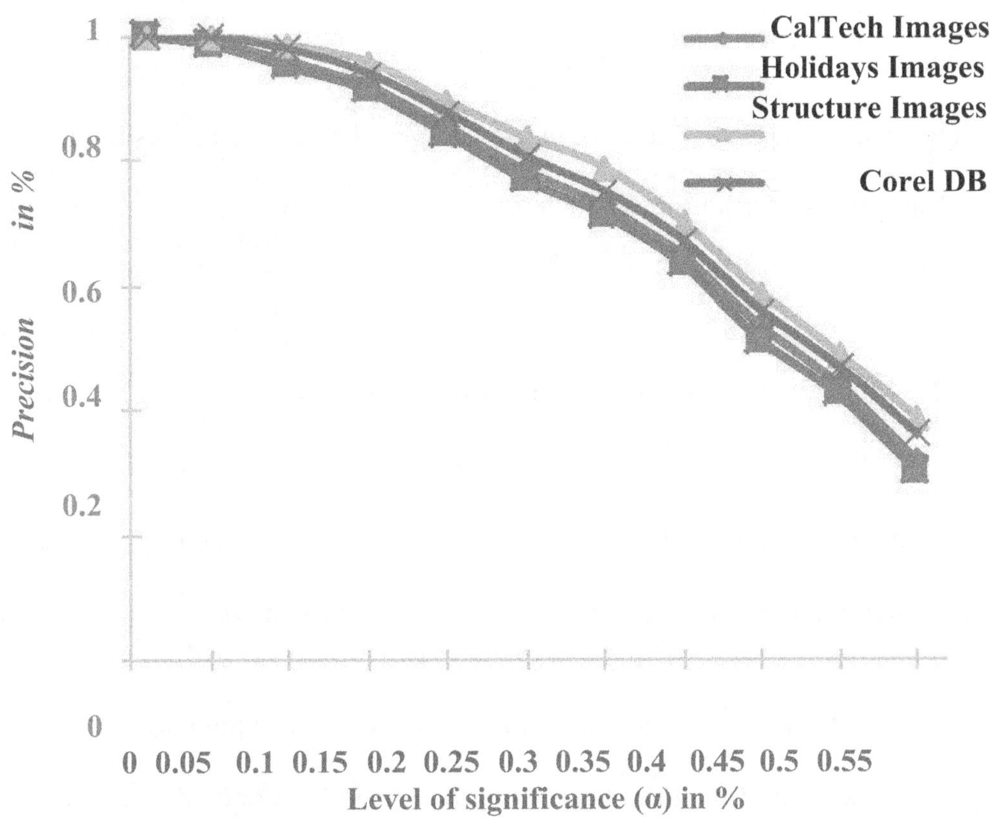

Figure 5.7: Line Graph: Threshold (t) vs. Mean Average Precision Scores

To explore the attributes of the system, the precision, recall, and F-measure are computed using the expressions given in Equations (4.5), (4.6), (4.7), and (4.8) of the Chapter 4 for the results obtained at various significance levels; and those are graphically represented as in Figure 5.7. It is observed from the experiments that the proposed system yields better results to structure images while compared to those of the textured or semi-textured, because the structured images are segmented into various regions according to its nature, the image data become homogeneous and so the mean and variances computed for the shapes are more precise than the textured or semi-structured images. Also, the semi-textured images are mixed data types than the fine texture. In the case of semi-textured images, the images are not segmented so the data are mixed (non-homogeneous or heterogeneous). The graph, also, reveals that the F-measure score decreases monotonically while the significance level increases. The increase of the significance level causes the system to return more images. Thus, it facilitates the users to fix the level of significance according to their suit, so that the users can get a number of images as desired.

5.2.2 Multivariate Parametric Statistical Methods

To examine the statistical methods discussed in Chapter 3, which are implemented with the image database constructed in Chapter 4. A few of the images considered for the experiment are given here, for a sample, owing to space constraints.

The features of the query image are extracted region-wise, if it is structured, and that are compared with the features in the image feature database. The target images are identified and marked in the image database, based on the results obtained from the tests.

According to users' requirements of the number of same or similar images, the user can fix the level of significance of the tests. The proposed system matches and retrieves the same image (target and query images are same) from the image feature database for the level of significance at 0.001% (100% accuracy-same images); almost same images for 1% to 2% (98% accuracy) level of significance; similar images for the level of significance from 3% to 5%; related images for the level of significance from 6% to 8%. The selected images are indexed (ranked) from lowest to highest, i.e. in ascending order based on the test statistic values obtained. The image which corresponds to the first value in the indexed list is marked as target image and it is retrieved from the image database.

As discussed in the case of bivariate statistical methods, the input query image is performed pre-process, and then it is subjected for segmentation of shapes or structures, matching, indexing, and retrieval process. The shapes in the input query image are segmented into various regions. If the query image is colour, then the segmented colour image is converted into HSV colour space. The H, S, and V colour components are considered for the experiment. The proposed method identifies the number of shapes in the query image as discussed in [Seet14], and compares them with the number of shapes in the image feature database. Number of shapes in the query and target images are represented with π_q and π_t respectively. If it satisfies the condition expressed in Equation (5.1), the system proceeds to the retrieval process:

$$\left(\left(\frac{\pi_q}{\pi_t}\right)\times 100\right) \leq t_\alpha \qquad \text{... (5.1)}$$

where, t_α is a criterion for matching the objects in the images, and it is fixed at 20%; either the query image or the target image, which has lesser number of objects, is put in the place of numerator, and the other is put in denominator. The mean vector, M, and the covariance matrix, Σ, of the query image are computed as discussed in section 3.2 of the Chapter 3. The probability values, P_q, of each region of the query image are computed using the expression given in Equation (3.6) of the Chapter 3. The probability values, mean vector and covariance matrix of the target image are considered from the feature database. The Chernoff distance measure expressed in Equation (3.5) of the Chapter 3 is applied to measure the distance between the query and target images.

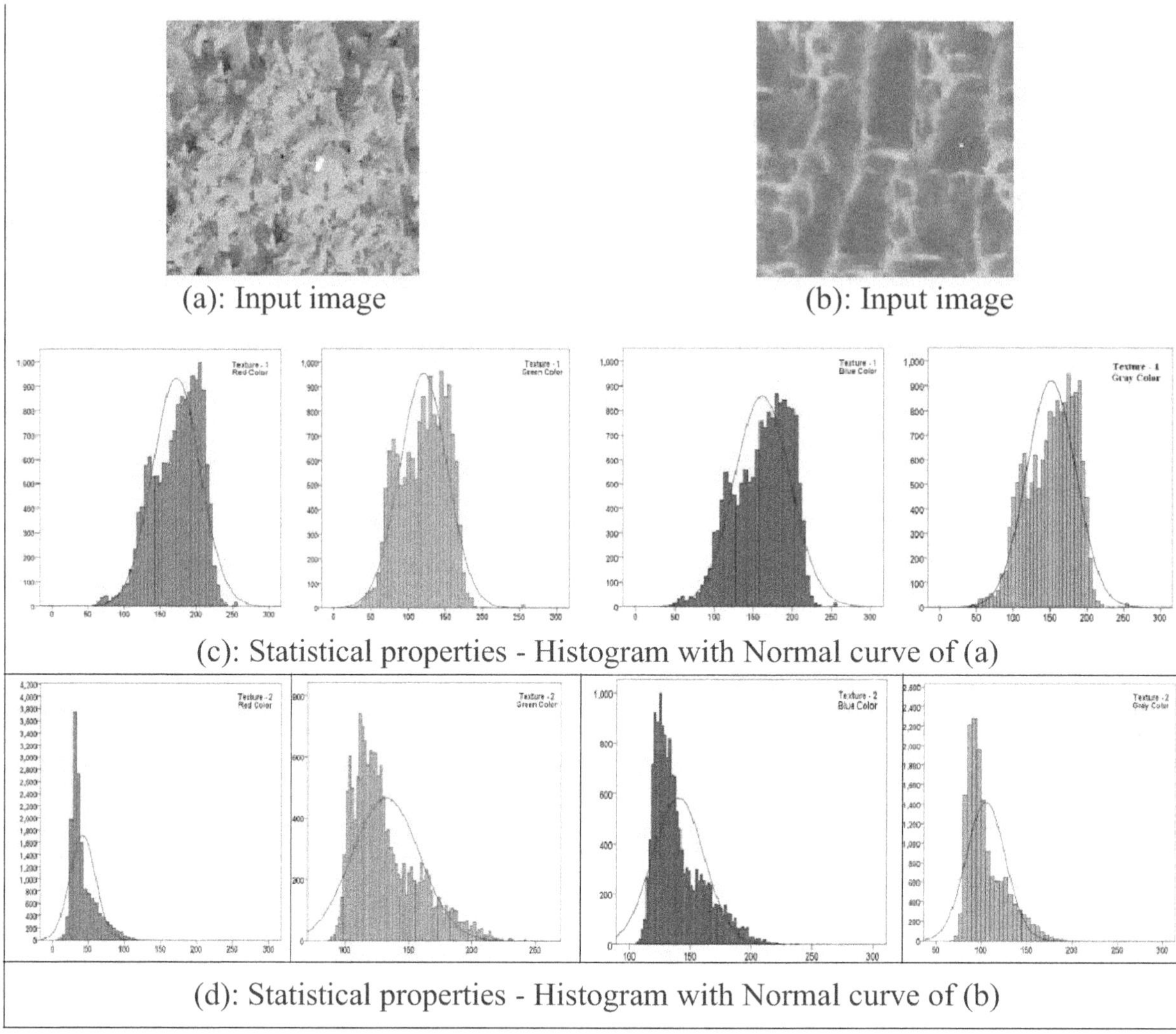

Figure 5.8: Texture images and their distributional properties

Figure 5.9: Output of the pre-processing technique: row 1: noisy images; row 2 - denoised

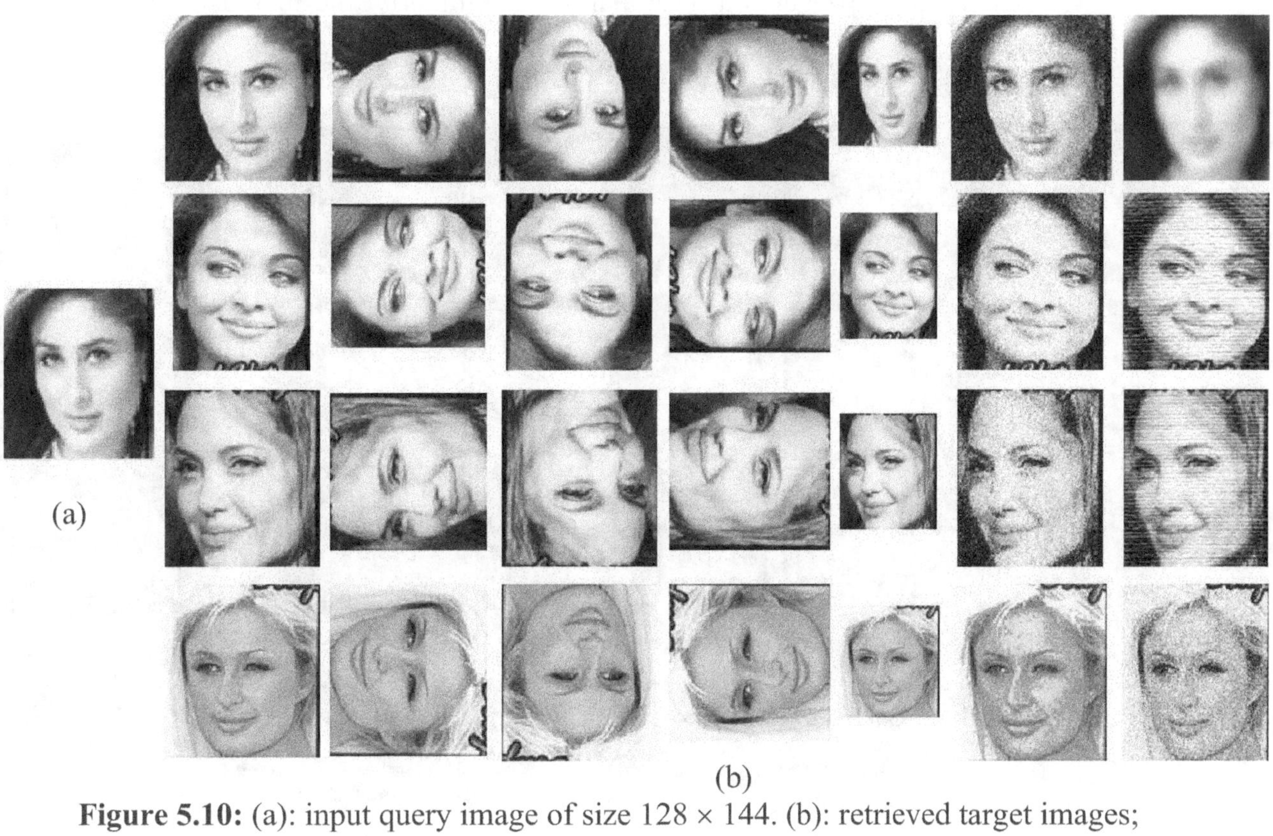

Figure 5.10: (a): input query image of size 128 × 144. (b): retrieved target images; column 1: actual images of size 128 × 144 retrieved target images; column 2: images in column 1 are rotated either clockwise or anticlockwise through 90°; column 3: images in column 1 are rotated clockwise through 180°; column 4: images in column 1 are rotated either clockwise or anticlockwise through 270°; column 5: scaled images; column 6:

noisy images of column 1; column 7: different types of noisy images

In order to validate the proposed method, a number of structured images are considered for the experiment; a few of them are presented in this section. The image given in Figure 5.10(a) is inputted as a query to the method. The method retrieves the images presented in row 1 of the Figure 5.10(b) at the level of significance, 0.05; specifically the method retrieves the first four images of the row 1 at the level of significance 0.01 or lesser, whereas it retrieves the 5th image (scaled) in the same row at the level of significance 0.03 or lesser; the last two images (noisy) are retrieved at the level of significance 0.05 or lesser. At the level of significance, 0.10 or lesser, the method retrieves the images in row 2; as in the case of row 1, the images in row 2 are retrieved at various significant levels but less than 0.10. Similarly, the images in rows 3 and 4 are retrieved at the level of significance 0.15.

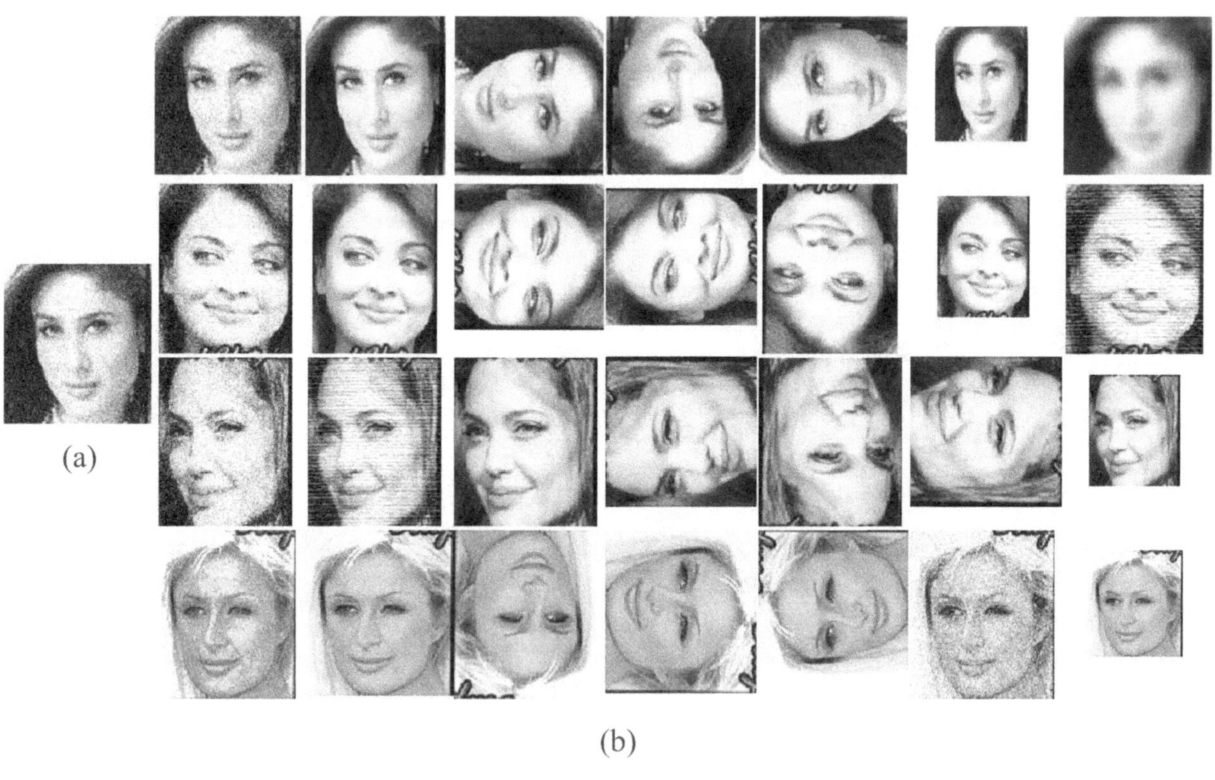

(a) (b)

Figure 5.11: (a): query image of size 128 × 144; (b): retrieved target images

In order to cross-check the efficiency of the proposed method, noisy version of the input image considered in the Figure 5.11(a) is inputted to the method. The images presented in row 1 are retrieved, at different significant levels, have been presented in columns 2-8 of the Figure 5.11(b). The images retrieved are presented in an order, in which they have been retrieved, in the Figure 5.11(b).

Figure 5.12: Column 1: input query images; columns 2-7: retrieved target images

The images presented in column 1 of the Figure 5.12 are given as input query to the system, and the retrieved images are presented in columns 2 - 7. The images in row 1 are retrieved at the level of significance 0.08; images in rows 2 and 3 are retrieved at the level of significance 0.12, while the images in row 4 are retrieved at 0.10. The images in row 5 are retrieved, when the level of significance is fixed at 0.15; at the significance level 0.17, the images in row 6 are retrieved.

Moreover, the experiment is conducted on Holidays image dataset at different significance levels the input query and target images are presented in Figure 5.13. The images in columns 2 - 4 are retrieved at the level of significance 0.1, while the images in columns 5 and 6 are retrieved at the level of significance 0.15. At the level of significance 0.18, the images presented in column 7 are retrieved. The images in column 1 of the Figure 5.13 are given as input query image to the proposed method.

(a)	(b)

Figure 5.13: Column 1: input query images; columns 2 - 7: retrieved target images

An attempt is made, on a trial basis, to test the appropriateness of the proposed method for the images captured by satellites, such as water-bank and forest images. For a sample, a few of them are presented in Figs. 5.14 and 5.15. The proposed method retrieves the images in row 1 of the Figure 5.14(b) at the level of significance, 0.12; the images in rows 1 and 2 are retrieved at the level of significance, 0.18; the images in rows 1, 2 and 3 are retrieved while fixing significance level at 0.22. The average percentage of the precision and recall values are presented in Table

Though the proposed retrieval method is not developed exclusively for satellite image retrieval, it gives good results. The same image is fed to the orthogonality measure given in Equation (3.10) of the Chapter 3. The method retrieves the images in column 2 of the Figure 5.15 while fixing θ at seven or less than seven degrees; images in columns 3, 4, and 5 are retrieved when θ is at eighteen degrees; images in columns 6 and 7 are retrieved when θ is at twenty six degrees.

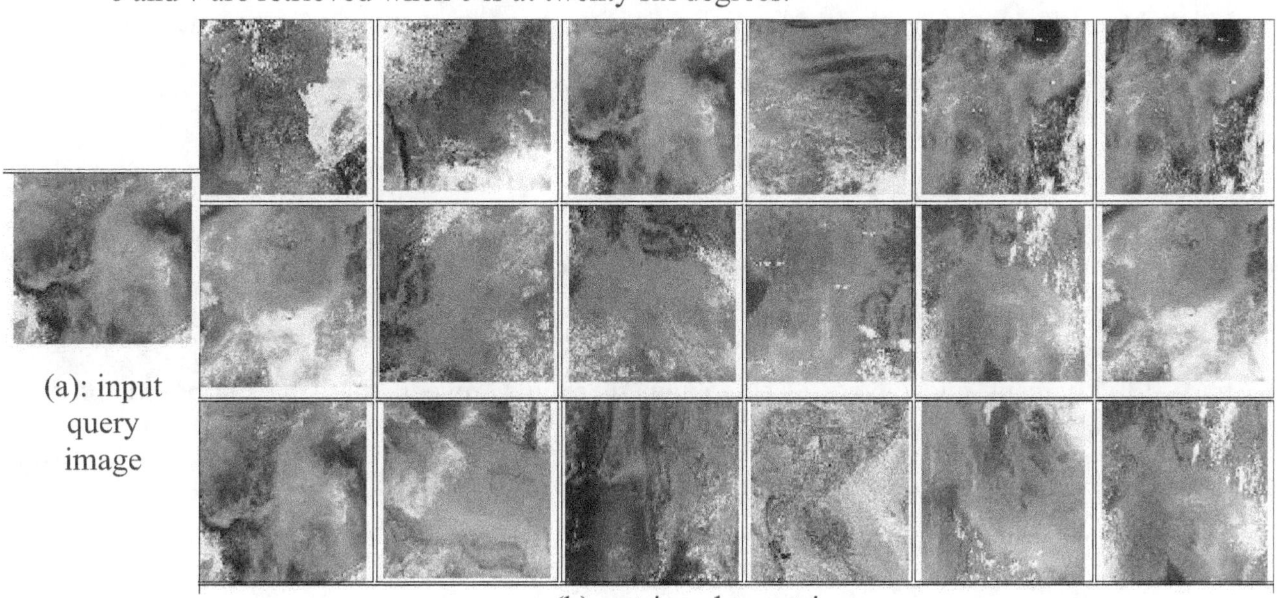

(a): input query image

(b): retrieved target image

Figure 5.14: Satellite images - Water-bank images; (a): input query image; (b): retrieved target image

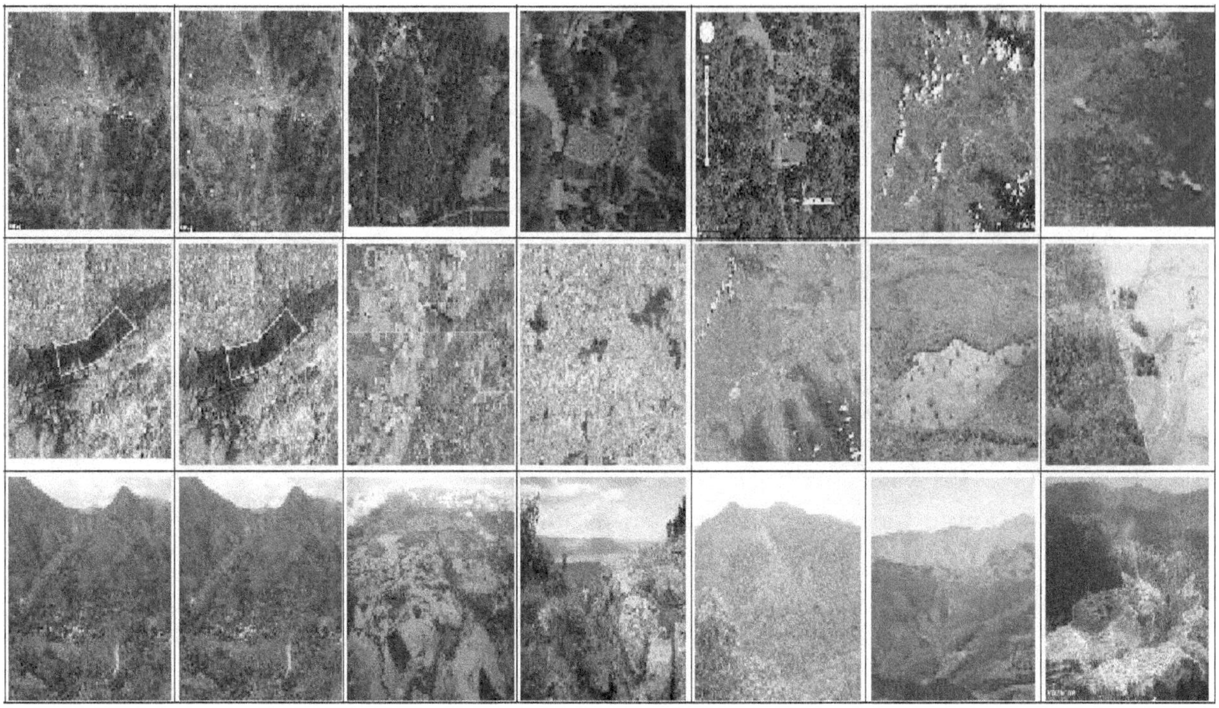

Figure 5.15: Satellite images - Forest images; column 1: input query images; columns 2 - 7: retrieved target images

In order to evaluate and validate the performance of the proposed method, the obtained results are compared with those of the existing methods: Orthogonal Polynomial (OP) [Kris13], Kullback-Liebler distance (KLD) [Suma12], Bhattacharyya distance (BD) [Yang13], and Mahalanobis distance (MD) [Hoi10] in terms of F_β-measure, which is computed by taking average of the precision and recall values of the retrieved results. The average of the precision and recall values are obtained at the level of significance (α) 0.15 percent and above. The obtained results reveal that the proposed method outperforms the existing methods. But, this paper takes account of texture or semi-texture images, structure images, and various types of satellite images. Average of the precision, recall, and F_β-measure values are calculated for various methods:

In every research work, evaluation of proposed system is a significant step decide if the suggested methods satisfy the requirement or not. However, based on application domain, there are such metrics used for evaluation purposes and these metrics reflect the goodness of proposed methodology in every research works. Hence, for retrieving purposes, Precision (P), Recall (R), F-Measure, and Accuracy (AC) are the best metric used commonly to evaluate the CBIR systems.

Table 5.2: Evaluation of Proposed System for Caltech Dataset.

S.No	Image Category	No. of Relevant Images in DB	Total Images Retrieved	No. of Relevant Images Retrieved	P	R	F-Measure	ACC
1	Ketch	12	12	12	1.0	1.0	1.00	100
2	Aeroplane,	10	12	10	0.8	0.8	0.82	84%
3	Faces	10	10	9	0.9	0.9	0.92	91%
4	Piano	8	8	8	1.0	1.0	1.00	100
5	Bikes	8	10	8	0.8	0.8	0.82	86%
6	Leopard	10	11	10	0.9	0.9	0.90	92%
7	Bonsai	8	8	8	1.0	1.0	1.00	100
8	watch	8	10	6	0.8	0.8	0.82	82%

Table 5.3: Evaluation of Proposed System for INRAI Dataset.

S.No	Image Category	No. of Relevant Image	Total Images Retriev	No. of Relevant	P	R	F-Measure	ACC
1	Ketch		8	8	1.00	1.00	1.00	100%
2	Aeroplane,		10	8	0.84	0.82	0.80	85%
3	Faces		10	8	0.84	0.82	0.84	85%
4	Piano		8	8	1.00	1.00	1.00	100%
5	Bikes	8	12	8	0.78	0.79	0.77	74%
6	Leopard		10	8	0.84	0.86	0.82	85%
7	Bonsai		12	7	0.80	0.82	0.84	81%
8	watch		11	7	0.80	0.82	0.82	80%

Table 5.4 :The average precision results of the proposed method compared with the other standard retrieval methods.

Class	Proposed method	Orthogonal Polynomial	Kullback-Liebler	Bhattacharyya	Mahalanobis
Ketch	0.96	0.733	0.19	0.18	0.12
Aeroplane,	0.82	0.811	0.75	0.51	0.74
Faces	0.90	0.892	0.70	0.53	0.64
Piano	0.83	0.727	0.80	0.57	0.78
Bikes	0.87	0.871	0.75	0.69	0.81
Leopard	0.96	0.917	0.95	0.89	0.95
Bonsai	0.838	0.828	0.65	0.56	0.64
watch	0.96	0.951	0.90	0.78	0.95
Animal	0.99	0.828	1.00	0.98	0.99
Ins	0.755	0.632	0.75	0.61	0.70
Average	0.8883	0.830	0.820	0.701	0.812

Table 5.5 : The average recall results of the proposed method compared with the other standard retrieval methods.

Class	Proposed method	Polynomial	Kullback-Liebler	Bhattacharyya	Mahalanobis
Ketch	0.75	0.733	0.19	0.18	0.12
Aeroplane,	0.75	0.732	0.15	0.15	0.21
Faces	0.815	0.805	0.14	0.13	0.19
Piano	0.58	0.533	0.16	0.16	0.14
Bikes	0.62	0.600	0.15	0.16	0.13
Leopard	0.66	0.647	0.19	0.19	0.11
Bonsai	0.73	0.706	0.13	0.13	0.14
watch	0.85	0.848	0.18	0.19	0.13
Animal	0.75	0.726	0.20	0.20	0.10
Ins	0.62	0.585	0.15	0.14	0.17
Average	*0.7125*	*0.691*	*0.164*	*0.163*	*0.144*

algorithm with the GA has raised the quality of solution (weight) via the increase of the fitness number. This has helped in the improvement of the exploitation process when the searching process is being conducted. Clearly, the experimental outcomes are demonstrating the capacity of our proposed techniques in assisting the retrieval of the great amount of the relevant images to the query image.

Table 5.1: Performance of the Proposed Method with Other Existing Methods

Image Database	Proposed system (α is at 0.15 and above)				Orthogonal Polynomial				Kullback-Liebler				Bhattacharyya				Mahalanobis			
	Recall	Precision	F	Accuracy	Recall	Precision	F	Accuracy	Recall	Precision	F	Accuracy	Recall	Precision	F	Accuracy	Recall	Precision	F	Accuracy
CalTech &INRIA	0.9282	0.8152	1.5040	92.24	0.9015	0.7631	1.4171	88.12	0.8781	0.7293	1.3589	89.65	0.8523	0.6937	1.2970	84.25	0.8252	0.6817	1.2713	84.50
Corel	0.9298	0.8585	1.5693	91.50	0.9255	0.8039	1.4861	85.35	0.8182	0.7863	1.4265	85.40	0.7829	0.7736	1.3958	89.87	0.8095	0.6912	1.2816	89.10
Structure Images	0.9426	0.8991	1.6334	91.50	0.8149	0.7101	1.3119	85.50	0.8925	0.8413	1.5319	87.65	0.8579	0.8018	1.4624	82.15	0.7727	0.7491	1.3567	80.55
Satellite Images	0.7962	0.7698	1.3949	92.53	0.8267	0.7203	1.3308	88.50	0.7428	0.7259	1.3126	89.75	0.7186	0.7021	1.2696	84.50	0.6853	0.6482	1.1795	86.55

Time Complexity

A comparative study is performed, in order to evaluate the computational time complexity of the proposed method, with the existing methods: OP method, KLD, BD and MD measures. The method is implemented using Java SE 7 compiler with system specification, Intel Core i5-4440 processor based PC with 4GB DDR3 RAM. The time consumed by the proposed method for feature extraction, matching and retrieving the images is measured in seconds, and the obtained results are presented in Table 5.2. Though the proposed method requires time marginally more than the BD and MD measures, it is lesser than the KLD, and the proposed method yields better results in the retrieval rate. The marginal time taken by the proposed method is negligible, as compared with other existing methods, in terms of retrieval-rate and accuracy.

Table 5.2: Comparison of Computational Time Complexities

Time Consumption	Proposed method	OP	KLD	BD	MD
Feature extraction time	0.513 sec	0.798 sec	0.736 sec	0.975 sec	0.852 sec
Searching time	0.0438 sec	0.072 sec	0.060 sec	0.070 sec	0.691 sec

5.3 POSITION VECTORS AND ORTHOGONALITY

The same image is fed to the orthogonality measure given in Equation (3.10) of the Chapter 3. The method retrieves the images in column 2 of the Figure 5.15 while fixing θ at seven or less than seven degrees; images in columns 3, 4, and 5 are retrieved when θ is at eighteen degrees; images in columns 6 and 7 are retrieved when θ is at twenty six degrees.

Furthermore, to emphasize the efficiency and effectiveness of the proposed system, the Wall-Street Bull images presented in Figure 5.6 are included in the experiment for measuring the divergence between the images using the expression given in equation 3.10 of the Chapter 3. The obtained results are presented in Table 5.3. The obtained results strengthen that the proposed method is very effective and efficient compared to that of the existing methods.

Table 5.3: Angle (θ) between the tiger images

Vs.	T1	T2	T3	T4	T5	T6	T7
T1	00.00	07.25	09.53	14.05	18.54	20.22	21.95
T2	07.25	00.00	08.35	12.01	18.18	20.76	21.74
T3	09.53	08.35	00.00	12.53	17.33	18.07	21.17
T4	14.05	12.01	12.53	00.00	14.44	16.42	19.33
T5	18.54	18.18	17.33	14.44	00.00	12.63	16.90
T6	20.22	20.76	18.07	16.42	12.63	00.00	13.88
T7	21.95	21.74	21.17	19.33	16.90	13.88	00.00

5.4 DISCUSSION

In order to examine the proposed method, a manifold images have been included in the experiment. The retrieval results are compared with the Orthogonal Polynomial method, Kullback-Liebler, Bhattacharyya, and Mahalanobis distance measures. The OP method yields moderate results for the noised images compared to that of other images, because the Haar Wavelet is not tolerable for the images with noise. The OP method is time consuming, since it involves the computation of model coefficients, and genetic algorithm is used to find optimized weight for each feature. These lead to the computational complexity of the Orthogonal polynomial method.

In the case of Bhattacharyya distance the terms P_q and P_t are fixed to 1/2, whereupon it does not yield better results than the other existing methods because nature -- the structure and content -- of the images varies from image to image; so they can have an effect on P_q and P_t values. Thus, it is not rational to fix P_q to ½ in the context of automated image retrieval or analysis. As the BD is a special case of the CD, it leads to moderate results for all types of images while compared to the CD. But in the case of CD measure, the probability value of P_q is not chosen arbitrarily; instead it is computed according to the nature and structure of the images. Hence, the Chernoff distance measure leads to better results than the Bhattacharyya distance. Moreover, in the case of Bhattacharyya, there is a constraint that the images must be distributed to Gaussian process, whereas there is no such a constraint in the case of Chernoff distance, viz. the images may be distributed to Gaussian or other than the Gaussian or mixed or distribution free. Hence, the CD measure is more appropriate for automatic image retrieval when compared to the Bhattacharyya distance measure. As the image retrieval method is automatic, it is difficult to identify that the images follow which distribution.

CHAPTER 6

DISCUSSION AND CONCLUSION

6.1 GENERAL DISCUSSION

Though a number of methods are available for colour image retrieval systems using low-level and high-level image features, each method is concerned with a specific type of process either at low-level or high-level, and also complicated. The proposed system is invariant for rotation, scaling, and noise, since the query image is treated as a sample or population of the target image and vice-versa. But, at the same time, it is simple and efficient. The research work carried out in this thesis is aimed to obtain a common framework for colour image retrieval, based on the Bivariate and Multivariate statistical tests of hypotheses, orthogonality tests.

6.2 ADVANTAGES OF THE PROPOSED SCHEME

In the earlier works [Theo05], the block-wise sampling / segmentation technique is used. The block-wise sampling / segmentation technique does not give good results for the same image with transformed one. The corresponding blocks of query (actual) and target (transformed) images are not spatially matching, if the target image is transformed. So the earlier techniques fail to locate and retrieve the correct images. This problem is overcome in the proposed technique, since the query image or the target image is treated as a sample of one another. Since the proposed system uses the global distributional (query and target images) differences, it overcomes the existing drawbacks in the earlier systems. Also, the computational complexity is reduced considerably by adopting the multivariate tests of hypothesis.

If $CD(P_q, P_t) \leq 1\text{-}\alpha$, at the level of significance $\alpha = \Sigma \sqrt{P_q, P_t}$ then it is inferred that the query and target images are same or similar; otherwise, the two images differ. Based on the outcome of the inference, the matched images (same or similar) are marked and indexed in ascending order, and the indexed images are retrieved. The significance level, α, is fixed after conducting a rigorous experiment with various types of images, such as texture (both stochastic and periodic) and untexture or structure.

The proposed method, based on the CD measure, has three main advantages:

(i) It adapts itself to all types of images, i.e. the images follow either Gaussian or mixed or non-Gaussian process because *a priori* probabilities, P_q and P_t, of the query and target images play a noteworthy role in measuring the distance between them; The P_q and P_t are computed, based on the query and target images, they are not fixed to 1/2 as in BD.

(ii) In the case of BD, the *a priori* probabilities, P_q and P_t, of the query and target images are fixed to 1/2, which is optimal; so they must adhere to the Gaussian properties.

In the case of image retrieval, the *a priori* probability of the query image which matches with the target image is fixed to 1/2. It is biased because the image may or may not adhere to the Gaussian properties. In the case of fully automated image retrieval system, it is difficult to understand the nature or structure of an image without analysis; and it is not fair to fix the *a priori* probability of P_q to 1/2. Thus, the BD is not appropriate for all types of images; so it does not lead to a better result.

In the case of CD, the *a priori* probability of P_q is estimated according to the nature of the query image. So the proposed method works well for any type of images, even though they are distributed to either Gaussian or mixed or non-Gaussian random process or even if it is distribution free. Thus, the proposed method leads to better results than those of the existing methods.

6.3 SCOPE OF THE FUTURE WORK

There are many interesting topics in computer applications, such as image processing, computer vision, pattern recognition, data mining, etc. which need further research work. The proposed common framework based on the statistical tests of hypotheses and orthogonality test can be utilised to fulfil the current requirements.

The proposed common framework can be effectively utilised for extraction of features in managerial data, and retrieval of information for quick decision making. The proposed method can also be applied in the field of agricultural, medicine for extracting the features, and searching the information. It can also be extended for the multi-spectral satellite image retrieval.

www.ingramcontent.com/pod-product-compliance
Lightning Source LLC
LaVergne TN
LVHW082354200926
848481LV00012B/3566
9798232136819